BODY AND CELL

Body and Cell

Making the transition to cell church—a first-hand account

HOWARD ASTIN

MONARCH
B O O K S

First published by Monarch Books 1998

ISBN 1 85424 409 4

Editorial Office: Monarch Books,
Broadway House, The Broadway, Crowborough,
East Sussex TN6 1HQ

British Library Cataloguing Data
A catalogue record for this book is available
from the British Library.

Designed and produced for the publishers by
Bookprint Creative Services
P.O. Box 827, BN21 3YJ, England
Printed in Great Britain.

CONTENTS

To all members of St John's Bowling, many of whom think they're 'nowt special' but are.

FOREWORD

There is a huge interest in the cell church movement and I would suggest that any congregation of whatever denomination must read this book. It will help you think through structures and values and how to change from being an ordinary church with groups into a cell church and all that means.

In this exciting and personal book, Howard Astin asks two major questions. What will the church look like as we enter the new millennium? How can we be effective both as a community and in the way we evangelise?

Some of the answers to these questions are described through Howard's personal journey and that of his church, St John's, Bowling in Bradford, which in 1993 went through a remarkable transformation to become a church which is cell based in structure and vision. Howard has gone back to a biblical pattern of church and concentrates not just on the importance of small groups but shows how they are to be in balance with the wider congregation.

In this thoroughly practical book, Howard outlines his own journey, both theologically and experientially and, setting it in its Anglican context, the route taken by the congregation of St John's, Bowling. At the same time,

Howard gives sound, realistic teaching for other churches who might want to embark upon a similar pilgrimage.

Within these pages, Howard describes the rationale behind the cell structure and how it differs from a church with house groups. He also writes about the methods through which the cell concept was put to the church members, their initial reactions, the selection and training of leaders and how the groups themselves developed and changed. He admits it's not been all plain sailing and describes the frustrations involved and the attitudes of different people towards his church's paradigm shift.

Howard also provides a valuable international overview of the cell church movement. His own experience was initially inspired by American author, Ralph Neighbour who in the 1980s worked on and wrote about cell churches in Singapore. There is now a thriving cell church movement across Africa, Asia and South America with a notable example being Dr David Yonggi-Cho's Yoido Full Gospel Central Church in Seoul, South Korea which now numbers nearly a million members, and first adopted the cell approach in 1964. St John's, Bowling was one of the first churches to become a cell church in the United Kingdom and many others are now seriously considering making the change.

With its personal stories, useful diagrams and practical advice, this book will make a difference to any church which seeks to apply its content.

The new millennium will be a challenge for all of us and I hope that this book will help churches think of new ways of facing up to that challenge and how to find out what God has planned for his Church.

Laurence Singlehurst
Director, YWAM England.
March 1998

INTRODUCTION

In July 1993 we scrapped our house groups. In October 1993 we began meeting in cell groups. We did not realise what a revolutionary step we were taking. Scrapping the existing house groups was painful for some people as they could no longer meet weekly with friends in cosy clusters. For others it was a welcome relief not to have to struggle on any longer in groups they did not enjoy. Four years on, we have experienced both joy and pain but we remain committed to being a cell-group church. We would not go back.

There is much talk of 'cell groups' in the Church today, and it can be confusing. We naively believed in 1993 that many churches in Britain had cell groups. Indeed, many said they had. However, it soon became clear that for some, 'cell groups' were identical to our previous house groups; in other words, a group of people from a local church meeting mid week to study the Bible and pray, or 'have fellowship' together.

A true definition of a cell, however, *must* include growth. A cell must have the element of multiplication. Our human bodies are made up of cells, and those cells continually multiply. For a child to grow, the human cells must multiply. So within the Church a cell group must multiply. If cells do not multiply in our human bodies, we are dead! Surely the same applies to the Church? It is hardly a coincidence that the Church is referred to as the 'body' of Christ. We used to have mid-week groups that met together to study the Bible, pray and have fellowship. Now we have cell groups that, in addition to these activities, also aim to reach out and grow in number, so they can multiply from one group into two.

Like any other Church leader, I am tempted to adopt the latest trend that will bring Church growth. In recent years we have been excited by 'seeker services' developed in Willow Creek Church in Chicago, and much has been written and done in transferring the principles seen there to our culture here. Then there is the Alpha course, which some churches use with their whole congregation and others use to help those who have expressed an interest in Christianity. Other churches have seen church-planting as the way forward. Charlie Cleverley calls his book *Church Planting, Our Future Hope* because it seems so central to growth.[1] At least one new plant starts each week in the Anglican Church in England. Many churches have been greatly helped by one or other of these strategies.

In our four years of cell groups, we too have grown in numbers, but I am convinced that this is not really what cell-group church is all about. There is so much more. We must resist the temptation to adopt the cell structure as the next 'quick fix' to make the Church grow. That has not been our experience here. Rather, it has been difficult and painful to shift an existing church into this new structure.

Yet, it is worth it. It has been so exciting to see the church fellowship change, not only in its structure, but also in the thinking and values of the members. It has been wonderful to witness a seventy-year-old member no longer believing that it is someone else's job to reach out and tell others about Jesus but now having the confidence to chat with her neighbours and friends about her own relationship with the Lord. Likewise, it has been a joy to see so many take a hold of the truth of their self-worth in the Lord. Knowing they are accepted and loved by God has released them into venturing out to do so many things for the Lord, whether it is praying for others in their cell group or seeking to serve those around them in the community.

This book is the story of how we came to be a cell-group church and what it has meant to us. It's about what we have done and why we did it. It is also about what we have learned during these last four years. We want others to be enthused about cell-group church and be encouraged to take the next steps.

This is not a book just for Church leaders, but for every member who wants to see the Church giving glory to God within its fellowship and also as it reaches out into the community.

CHAPTER 1

WELCOME TO ST JOHN'S, BOWLING

You could be forgiven for not realising that St John's, Bowling, Bradford was different from any other lively Anglican church when you visit a Sunday service. You will not see the fundamental differences which make us a cell-group church here.

When you walk into either our 9 am or 11 am service, you will see the heading over the notice-board stating that St John's is a cell-group church. You may hear the reference to the children going out to their 'cell groups' after fifteen minutes of the worship service. During the sermon you may hear the suggestion that certain points could be discussed further and prayed through at the cell groups during the coming week.

But it is doubtful whether you would realise that for each service there is a different cell group responsible for welcoming at the door, for making and serving coffee, and for the ministry prayer time at the end of each service. You could be forgiven for believing that St John's, Bowling operates in much the same way as many churches across Britain.

However, it doesn't.

The cell group is the life of the church

To people joining the church through cell groups, it appears natural to meet in small groups mid week. However, for those who have been in the church for some years this can be a problem. The emphasis in the past has always been on meeting together in the church building for services. There are other meetings, but the Sunday service has traditionally been regarded as most important. Most, if not all, Church growth statistics across the denominations refer to attendance at Sunday services. But for the cell-group church, it's the group meetings that are central.

In simple terms, the mission statement of a cell-group church is 'to love God, to love others, and to love the lost'. Put another way, it is following John 13:34–35—'A new command I give you: Love one another. As I have loved you, so you must love one another. By this all men will know that you are my disciples, if you love one another.' Part of the agenda for the cell group is to 'love one another' as a natural progression from loving God. We love one another within the cell. Members of the cell are to minister to each other, to edify each other, to build each other up.

But this is not an end in itself. It was never intended to be, even though many of our house groups in the past have never got beyond this. We are to 'love one another' so that 'all . . . will know that you are my disciples'. Consequently, the cell group has the additional agenda to love people outside the group itself, with a view to the group increasing in numbers and eventually multiplying. This means evangelising.

Of course, not all the group members are called to be evangelists, but all are called to grow in discipleship and witness in the world. Cell groups are places where Christians are loved, ministered to and built up for their primary calling. The cells are then the centre of church life. They have both an inward emphasis and an outward emphasis (see Figure 1).

If a church follows a cell-group agenda the emphasis is transformed and the church moves from maintenance to mission. The phrase 'maintenance to mission' has become familiar over the last few years, especially through the writings of Robert Warren. We have spent too much time, money and energy in maintaining what we already have. We have been too busy keeping things going in the Church to witness effectively outwards to the community.

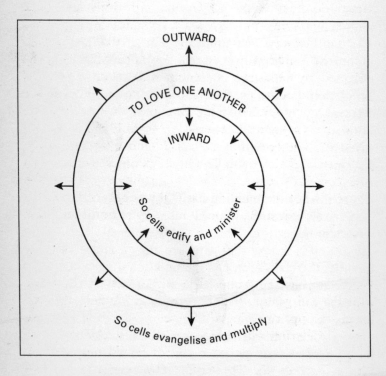

OUTWARD

TO LOVE ONE ANOTHER

INWARD

So cells edify and minister

So cells evangelise and multiply

Figure 1. The agenda of the cell group

The cell group is more than a home group

It has helped me to contrast the differences between a 'cell-group church' and a 'church with house groups'. The following list is a rough guide and a generalisation. Nevertheless, it does show the change of perspective which was needed not just for me or the church leadership, but for the whole membership of St John's, Bowling.

Cell-group centred/building centred

For too long, people have equated the Church with the church building. Maybe in Britain this stems from the visual dominance of our Gothic cathedrals and large church buildings, or the tacit acceptance by Christians all down the ages of the insidious belief that God dwells in church buildings in a special way. This view is widely accepted by God-fearers, people who retain a residual belief in the existence of God but do not consider themselves accountable to him. Even some Christians who know that they are the 'temple of the Holy Spirit' believe the same. The cell-group church demonstrates at a foundational level that God cannot be confined in this way. Although most Christians would readily accept that the Church is not the building but is the people of God, it is easy to imply just the opposite view by our attitudes, talk and actions.

Cell-group driven/programme driven

We do not have any activities in our church that compete with the cell groups. Church life either happens through the cell groups or it doesn't happen at all. Even when we were considering whether we could use an Alpha course we delayed it until we were sure it would not compete with cell-group life. The danger always was to have an additional 'centralised' programme as the main way in for

CELL-GROUP CHURCH	CHURCH WITH HOUSE GROUPS
Cell-group centred	Building centred
Church is cell-group driven	Church is programme driven
Cell groups are central	House groups exist chiefly for nurture, Bible study and fellowship
Focus is cell group	Focus is Sunday service
Outward looking	Inward looking
Decentralised for ministry, evangelism, etc	Centralised with ministry teams, evangelism team
Many lay leaders	Emphasis on professional leaders
Removes clergy/laity division	Reinforces clergy/laity division
Many points of entry (ie all groups)	Few points of entry (eg services, Alpha, etc)
Membership = cell group	Membership = electoral roll (for Anglicans) or church service attendance
All members are in cell group	House group is optional extra for members

Figure 2. Contrasting church models—rough guide[2]

new members to join the church, rather than have a tool that could be used to aid the cell groups in their evangelism and growth. We do now use Alpha, but in a way that allows people to join existing cells.

When no 'Bright and Light Party' was organised centrally by the church leadership for the children on

Hallowe'en, the elders redirected people's complaints to the leaders of the children's cell groups, who in future years organised the activity within their cell-group agendas. It is so easy to revert to a centralised programme. Some of us who have been Christians for years need a complete change of attitude, a change in the way we think church should be structured, to allow God to move by his Spirit through the cell-group life.

Cell groups are central/house groups are secondary

Our old house groups tended to be inward looking. There was the occasional house group with evangelistically gifted leaders which did grow and sometimes multiplied into two groups, but this was unusual. We generally used house groups to 'look after' members of the church. It was a holding process. Groups were primarily pastoral, there to help Christians to be nurtured, to grow in their knowledge of the Bible, and to be supported by other Christians.

There is nothing wrong with any of that. But over the years the Christian Church in this country has lost its natural (or rather supernatural) evangelistic cutting edge. Evangelism is seen as something to be done only by those who have the specific gift. The cell-group agenda brings back the vision of the early disciples to witness and to 'speak of what they had seen and heard'—their experience of God in their daily lives.

Focus is cell group/focus is Sunday service

This really does mean it is more important for a church member to be at the cell group than to be at the Sunday service. The Sunday service is still important for teaching and for celebration, but the fundamental life of the church is not found there. Rather, it is found at the cutting edge of personal relationships within the cells. The prayer ministry largely happens in the cell, the application of God's word happens in the cell, the intercessory prayer happens within the cell. All this is on a much more intimate level than can ever be achieved in a large gathering of people. This is where people's values are changed.

Outward looking/inward looking

We tried to be outward looking in the past. It was so difficult. When we met together in house groups the emphasis invariably became one of making the members feel better. Few of our church members really believed that God wanted to use *them* to bring another person to faith. Many did not even have close relationships with any non-Christians. Sometimes this was the church's fault in having so many meetings. There was no time to nurture relationships with family, friends, workmates and neighbours. The common belief was that if God was to speak significantly into another person's life, he would use someone else to do it—usually the preacher at a guest service. It has been exciting now to see people come to know that God wants to use *them* to be effective witnesses for him day by day. However, not everyone at St John's has grasped this yet. Some of us still do not *really* believe this truth. We need further re-educating, renewing and reviving in this.

Decentralised/centralised

Perhaps this is the main reason God is calling churches to become cell-group churches. At St John's we first saw the potential of cells as points of numerical growth. However, the longer we have had cell groups, the more we have seen the potential (and necessity) for 'every-member ministry' working through the cells. No longer do we have to rely on the specialised teams ministering to people at the end of the Sunday services. Nor do we have to rely on those specially gifted in evangelism to reach out into the community.

It is wonderful now to see 'ordinary' members of a cell praying with people at the end of Sunday services. Each adult cell is included on the rota for this responsibility. Even the newest cell member will be involved, accompanying a more experienced member to pray for others. More of this ministry goes on in the cells themselves. Cell members may also minister to each other in twos or threes outside the cell-group meeting setting. Yes, this has needed training, encouraging and correcting, but it has been liberating. In an area like ours where many people suffer from low self-esteem, they have not only been encouraged by experiencing God's love, but also by being used by him to help others.

Many lay leaders/emphasis on professional leaders

Fifty people went to our last leaders' conference. Just a few were missing. Out of an adult congregation of almost 200, we therefore have one quarter who are already leaders. Some lead adult groups, some lead youth groups or children's groups. All are leaders and all are lay. Perhaps it's because they saw quickly I was no omni-competent vicar that we have moved so readily to this delegation of leadership! Perhaps it's because one of my main leadership qualities is delegation!

However, I like to believe that it is also because God would have it so. Our model for leadership must be Jesus, and his method of training was one of apprenticeship. He took the disciples with him and they saw what he did. He then sent them out to do the same (Luke 9:1–9; 10:1–24). He taught them about the paradox of being master and servant (John 13:12–17). He commissioned them, promising his presence with them by the Spirit (Matthew 28:18–20). So in the cell-group church, there is apprenticeship training for leadership by setting example, delegating and commissioning.

Removes clergy/laity division/reinforces clergy/laity division

This links to the last point and asks fundamental questions concerning the role of clergy today. What is ordination? What is the ordained person called to do in the life of the Church? An increasing number of clergy are unsure what their role is, and more churches do not have a full-time leader. We need to reappraise the minister's task. The clergy still have a vital role to play, but today important new emphases require a new role. We need to train the laity in such things as pastoral care, prayer ministry, evangelism and the understanding of God's word. We will deal with this matter further in chapter 4.

Many points of entry/few points of entry

For many years we had a fairly successful 'basics' group that was similar to the modern Alpha. Nevertheless, we always had problems transferring people from that group to house groups. We tried every which way. Sometimes the basics group became a house group, using the existing leaders or using imported leaders. Sometimes we split the group, linking these new members with existing house groups. Each attempt seemed to be fundamentally flawed in one way or another and we often lost people in the transition.

Our emphasis is now on entry through the existing cell groups. The reason for this is the priority of relationships. Perhaps we have moved from a stance where new believers 'believe therefore belong' to the point where they 'belong therefore believe'. That is to say, they stay because a strong relationship has been built with other Christians. In the main they are attracted by the Christ they have seen in someone else, and come to believe in him as a continued revelation from God takes place. It may be that this has always been so, but our church structures in the past have often emphasised the opposite. Alpha courses, guest services and the like can still be entry points at St John's, but now they exist only because they enhance the evangelistic thrust of the cell-group members through their relationships.

Membership = cell group/membership = church roll or church service

It is difficult to know who is a member of the church. For some years I have accepted that it does not mean just those on the electoral roll of St John's (the Anglican 'membership' list). We have had some who are happy to belong to St John's, Bowling but who are slightly wary of belonging to the Church of England. (No doubt they read the newspapers!) They have not put their names on the electoral roll. It is difficult to say that they are not members of the church. We have seen people who arrive on Sunday, but nothing is seen or heard of them apart from for that hour or so. Maybe they are members of the Church of Christ, but are they also members of the church fellowship here at St John's, Bowling?

The Bible describes the Church, among other things, as 'the body of Christ' (1 Corinthians 12). It is difficult to see how someone can be a member if they are not actually joined to other parts of the body. Is standing next to someone and singing a hymn 'joining'? The cell church emphasises relationship. Of course, for some becoming a member is a slow process. They may prefer (for a time at least) the anonymity of just coming to the services and not building relationships. However, we are ultimately called to be part of the body of Christ and in relationship with each other. Therefore we are accountable to each other and responsible for each other. When a little finger hurts, we all hurt; when the nose rejoices, we all cheer! This is the real relationship of the local body of the Church. We shall look at this question of relationship in more depth in the next chapter.

All members are in cell group/house group is optional

It follows from all this that it's impossible for a person to be fully involved in the life of our church without also being in a cell. Church life goes on through the cells and everything revolves around the cells. We have very few people who attend St John's who are not in cells. The groups are not viewed as optional extras. The practical outworking of this is that it is very difficult for a person to be adequately cared for and supported if they do not belong to a cell. No one is forced to join a cell, but they are frequently invited to join.

The cell-group meeting

If visitors to St John's would not notice a great difference by turning up to a Sunday service, hopefully they would see the difference when they attended the cell-group meeting. There is a specific structure to the meeting. There is a different dynamic in our cell groups now from the house groups of years ago. So what actually happens in a cell-group meeting?

First of all, it should be remembered that the cell group is not just the cell-group *meeting*. If the cell is really based on relationships, then those relationships must exist and be worked out beyond this meeting. Our cells meet weekly, but that really is not enough to further a deep relationship of trust, support and commitment in which people truly learn to love one another. The constant challenge to our cell-group members is whether they are involved in each other's lives. Does membership just begin and end with attendance at the meeting? Or do they seek each other out on a Sunday at the service? Are they involved in each other's lives outside the meeting by chatting on the phone? Do they ever have a meal together outside the group night? Do they rally to each other's aid when someone is in difficulty? Would they think of calling someone else in their group first when they find themselves in difficulty? The acid test of the success of a group is the depth of relationships among its members.

Our experience is that this does not happen easily. In many ways it is 'counter culture'. In our working-class area, when troubles arise the family is usually the first natural port of call, often to the exclusion of all others. Sometimes people do not automatically mix together by entering each other's homes. Nevertheless, we are being called to demonstrate this love for one another to our community and this in itself is a powerful tool of witness to the love of Christ.

The meeting itself is central. It is the regular meeting of Christians to demonstrate their love for God, their love for each other, and their love for the lost. Back in 1993 we began following the structure for our cells outlined by Ralph Neighbour in his guide to cell-group churches. They are the four Ws in Figure 3. Four years later, we still stick to this structure, though hopefully with flexibility and creativity, and we have added a further dimension to it.

Probably the most unwelcome part of the meeting format is the **Welcome**—the ice-breaker to get people involved. Here is a fundamental difference between a house group and a cell-group meeting. Right at the beginning it acknowledges that there may be newcomers present. It implies that there are things we do not know about each other. It emphasises that everyone in the group needs to be involved in the meeting right from the start. In any setting when people meet together, those who are naturally outgoing and extrovert dominate the conversation. The quieter ones stay silent and uninvolved.

W	1.	**WELCOME**: an ice-breaker to get people involved.
I	2.	**WORSHIP**: songs, readings, meditations, etc.
N	3.	**WORD**: the application of last Sunday's sermon. This should end with prayer for individuals so application takes effect.
D:	4.	**WORKS**: the vision for the group to reach out to our φ*ikos* (a Greek word meaning 'household'—eg family, friends, work-mates, neighbours we spend quality time with each week).

Figure 3.

The ice-breaker aims to get *everyone* relating to each other from the word go.

If there is a newcomer, or someone who is especially shy, then they should not be made to feel uncomfortable. Something is needed just to get people talking—for example, 'Which TV programme has given you the most pleasure in the last week?' However, for a group that has been meeting together for some time and which has not had a newcomer for a period, a more intimate ice-breaker is appropriate. That may invite people to share something of a more personal nature, such as, 'What is the most significant thing that has happened to you over the last week?' The leadership needs training to know which ice-breaker to pick.

Over the years, some of the groups have been very imaginative in their ice-breakers. They have included party games or have followed the pattern of quiz nights down at the pub. Some activities have been so spiritually charged that God has broken in by his Spirit to direct members of the group to pray for each other before the meeting 'proper' begins. However, it is vital that relationships are formed or renewed as the meeting starts.

Some people who have been in the church for many years find the ice-breaker part quite difficult. Is it just our British culture that makes us rather reticent or leaves us with a desire to be more of a spectator than a participant? The old joke about the Church being rather like a football match still holds—those badly in need of a rest being watched by a far greater number badly in need of exercise! A change of attitude, or 'paradigm shift', in our thinking enables us to get involved together from the start so that our groups become places where it is easy for newcomers to feel at home.

We then move on to **Worship**. I doubt if we are the only church that does not have enough musicians to go round. The majority of our groups do not have resident worship leaders. We therefore have had to be even more creative, and the result has been a pleasure to see. Some of the apparently more unlikely people have discovered a gift in leading others in worship. This has not always been in music. Some have used tapes, both to listen to or to sing along with. Others have used readings or meditations, or have called on other members to participate by, for instance, calling out some of the names of God and praising him for that aspect of his character. Perhaps group members have not known the names of God, so the leader gives out slips of paper so that each person can share an aspect of praise.

It is vital that we worship God early in the meeting. It is because of him that the group is coming together. It is he who has revealed himself to the group members. It is he who has brought us into the 'body'. Of course, it is literally vital to worship, because during this time God can bring life—vitality—to the whole meeting. People arrive with their minds full of the activities of the day, the problems that surround them, or tensions about things ahead. Through worship, they become people who start to see their lives in the context of a God who loves them and accepts them and wants to lead, guide and empower them.

It is because of the worship that the next section of the meeting takes on a new relevance. This is the **Word**. It's here again that the cell-group meeting and the house-group meeting part company. We do not do a Bible 'study'. Rather, we apply the teaching of the Bible into our lives by applying the points raised in the previous Sunday's sermon. This invariably centres around one or two passages of the Bible, but the question is, how does it relate to our lives? What do we actually need to do about it?

For St John's this has been one of the most exciting parts of the transition from house group to cell group. Some of our house groups of the past also focused on application, but now there is the added element of cell members helping each other to apply God's word on the basis of their strong relationships. These two elements— the specific focus on application and the encouragement of deeper relationships—make the Bible come even more alive. God wants to speak into our lives and enable them to change. If we get to the end of this part of the meeting without there being some prayer for individuals, we've missed what God was wanting to do.

Of course we need to understand what the Bible is saying, and to know what it means. This is dealt with in the sermon. But if the passage is difficult to understand, further discussion with the preacher is encouraged, usually at coffee time on a Sunday morning. Misunderstanding can be dangerous and lead to false application. Nevertheless, we have found that it is important not to be distracted from the basic fact that God wants his word to be applied; to be life-giving to us.

For some of our leaders, mainly those who have been leaders of our house groups in the past, this has been a stumbling block. They have wanted to conduct a Bible study with little application as they did in our previous house groups. Or they have been tempted to rehash most of the sermon and to discuss again the reasoning behind the resultant points of application. Of course, sometimes this is briefly necessary. Usually it is not! For other leaders it has been a point of liberation. They no longer need to feel theologically inadequate.

If there is an issue of theology in dispute, then they refer back to the preacher. The preacher has given the leader an outline of the sermon and has even suggested some of the points of application that could be covered. Much of the worry of leading groups is eradicated by this central principle. We no longer look for budding theological students to lead our groups. Instead, leaders are people who care for others and have the desire and ability to help others see how God's word applies to their lives.

The final part of the meeting is the **Works**. Perhaps this is a confusing title but at least it begins with 'W' and may be apt because it is hard work! For many of us, the hardest part of being a Christian is to maintain the vision to reach out to others who are not yet Christians. The group finishes its time together in the meeting with a look outwards.

The word *φikos* is often referred to by cell-church movement theoreticians. It's a word that occurs on many occasions in the New Testament and does not have a simple English translation. More than simply 'house' it can also mean 'household', but really it embraces those with whom we spend quality time each week, such as our friends, family, workmates and neighbours. Group members suggest names of people who they want to pray for to become Christians. People are prayed for specifically and over a long period of time. These same people may well be invited to cell meetings which are of a more social nature such as ten-pin bowling or a day trip to Fountains Abbey. They may be invited round for meals with some other group members and their *φikos*. The desire is for the group to grow and to multiply.

Only when the group is really 'loving one another' will the works become more than a chore. Will people really pray for friends of other group members unless they care deeply for that group member and feel some of the burden that person feels for their *φikos* member? Isn't it a basic principle that we pray earnestly for those we care for? I have always found it difficult to pray for 'Emily's great aunt Beatrice' if I've never really got on with Emily and I've never met Beatrice. This is a new dimension for most of us, and it is still a great challenge.

Would I have prayed for Paul, I wonder, if I had been a Christian at Thessalonica? When he says, 'Pray for us' (1 Thessalonians 5:25), would I have done so unless I had actually met Paul and cared for him? When Paul himself gives his long list of greetings in Romans 16, his relationship with them comes through loud and clear: 'my fellow-workers'; 'my dear friend'; 'my relatives'; 'whom I love in the Lord'; 'who has been a mother to me'. God is calling us to move beyond praying through a list of names to praying for those with whom we have a relationship. Our groups are still learning this. It is easy to revert to the list without making the effort to develop the relationship with the concerned group member or the person being prayed for.

It is possible to 'do all the four Ws' and still miss the point! In Figure 3 above, embracing all the four components of the meeting is the **Wind**. After our groups had been running for a year or so we realised that sometimes we were so structure-bound that we did not allow God to move. The wind of the Holy Spirit must be allowed to blow through each meeting. We have found that sometimes he wants to break in even before we have broken the ice! So he makes his presence felt in the ice-breaker. Sometimes he transforms the worship so that the time allocated to this has to be extended. Sometimes the application of the word is so deep that some of us are thankful that we started with coffee because there was no time at the end! Maybe God wanted us to devote the whole meeting to looking outwards, as we have done enough looking inwards over the previous weeks, and any more just at that point would have been navel-gazing.

It is vital to rely on God. The structure of the meeting is no more a guarantee of life in the meeting than the structure of the cell church is a guarantee of life within the church body as a whole. We have been reminded time and time again that God is the one who gives life. God is the one who renews, and God is the one who brings about new things.

As the visitor comes to St John's, Bowling and begins attending cell-group meetings, he or she will start to see that being a cell-group church is something different. It is a new way of 'being church'. It is a new way of life for Christians.

CHAPTER 2

BEGINNINGS

I arrived at St John's, Bowling in 1988. The church was wonderful! Of course it had its problems, but so many of the members seemed open to all that God wanted to do in and through them. It was and is less middle class than many churches. Most members were 'unchurched' prior to joining us. Some were rough and ready people. I realised this when, a week or so after my arrival, I went to a conference with a few of them. One couldn't sleep in the guest house because he was used to sleeping rough, so he slept under the pier! I quickly got used to people walking out of services for a smoke—they called it a breath of fresh air! I even got to know the insides of prisons as I visited church members who were detained for a period. This was a real inner-city church and I loved it.

The church was built in 1842 for the workers of Bowling Iron Company. The Company was shamed into erecting the building because many workers were cramming into the small home of a lady called Sally week by week for worship and prayer. They were visited by a clergyman from Bradford Cathedral. The Anglican church now stands in an imposing position looking down over Bradford, a mile from the city centre on the south-east side.

The parish is geographically quite small, covering about

two square miles, with about 6,000 people living in 2,500 dwellings. It is not an area of great beauty; a third of the parish is industrial. There is some feeling of community in the area, as you can tell by standing in the queue at the post office on pensions morning—you should hear the gossip! Nevertheless, this sense of community is nothing like it was before the heart of the parish was ripped out when a three-lane dual carriageway was built next to the church in the 1970s.

I took over from a vicar who had worked there for twenty-six years. He had led the church along a sometimes stormy path to charismatic renewal in the early 1970s. He had gradually involved more and more of the congregation in the day-to-day ministry and teaching. They no longer relied on the supposed omnicompetence of the vicar. An eldership had been formed to spearhead strategy, and house groups had begun. These were called 'fellowship groups' and met weekly as holding and pastoring environments for existing members of the congregation. They were well attended, but often inward-looking and stagnant or at best 'comfortable'.

Nevertheless, it was a good foundation to build on. As the Spirit moved in the 1970s and early 1980s there was an important shift in the ministry from a group of gifted, experienced elders to the less experienced 'fellowship group' leaders. People did not rely solely on seeing the vicar (and/or the elders) for advice, prayer and counselling. They began to accept that God could and did work through group leaders to meet their felt needs. The move to this was often slow, not least because some leaders struggled to grasp their authority under God for this aspect of leadership. There were set-backs when some leaders overreached themselves or mistook exercising their delegated authority for doing their own thing. Then the group members would again seek out those tried and tested in such matters—the vicar and the elders.

By the early 1990s, the leadership of the church had been restructured, the building had been restored, and we had planted a church in the community centre on the other side of the dual carriageway. Many members were in fellowship groups where they received nurture and pastoral care. Other aspects of church life such as prayer, worship and evangelism were centralised. I was longing for them to be reaching out to their friends and relatives with the love of Christ in a more natural way than through small evangelistic teams, a city-wide mission, or the visiting evangelistic speaker at a guest service. But how? We were still frustrated and were desperately wanting to know 'what next?'

In addition, we faced what seemed to be the ineffectiveness of our nurturing of new Christians and bringing them into the full life of the church. There seemed to be an unfortunate pattern. New members stayed with us for two years or so and then started to drift away. Sometimes this was because they were challenged to give every part of their lives to the Lord Jesus. Many had come in wanting very much to meet with Jesus the Saviour so that the problems and difficulties in their lives would be sorted out. However, when Jesus had done that, they faced the challenge to follow him as Lord as well as Saviour, and even to change those parts of their lives that did not need such radical redemption. Many gave up at this point.

But this was not the full story, Some were not given the care, attention and help they needed. Others soon became frustrated because they could not find an area within the life of the church in which they could be useful. For example, they recognised that they were not going to be leaders, so what then was their calling? How did Jesus want to use them?

In the summer of 1992 a book came through my letter-box, sent from a pastor friend in the United States. It was called *Where Do We Go From Here?* by Ralph Neighbour.[3] The title seemed applicable. As my wife and I read it, we both knew without a shadow of doubt that God was calling us to lead the church towards the cell-group model. In other words, we were sure this was the answer to our question, 'What's next?'

I still recall the excitment I felt as I started to glimpse the possibilities of this radical approach to restructuring the church. Then I felt the enormity of the task ahead. Could we really see St John's change in this way? Could we move from its familiar structures to the cell-group model? Could we as an Anglican church implement this model without either compromising the model or our denominational distinctiveness? As we have done so, I have come to see that there are pastoral and evangelistic principles which relate to every church and never change whatever form of church government is favoured.

Cells can work in any church tradition

During my thirty years as a Christian I have spent time within a number of different denominations including Methodist, Baptist, Brethren, United Reformed and various house-church groupings. Perhaps it was being converted through a Christian Union camp that meant I have always appreciated mixing with Christians from across the denominational spectrum.

As a solicitor in my early twenties, I often witnessed the pain, frustration, injustice and conflict that many people suffered. I felt deeply concerned for them. Since entering the ministry, I have continued to feel a strong desire to show the relevance of God to people in these situations. Of course, God is in the good times too. He wants to enrich our everyday life with its amalgam of joy, pain, boredom, routine, frustration, excitement, disappointment, rest, conflict and the like. These are spiritual and pastoral principles that go beyond denominational boundaries. They are 'kingdom values'. They aim to make whole those within the church fellowship, and also to reach out to those who do not yet know Jesus' power in their lives.

Laurence Singlehurst, director of Youth With a Mission, speaks of kingdom values equalling cell values. He talks of the call to love God, to love each other and to love the lost. This is worked out by the cell group meeting with Jesus, so that every member grows as they minister to each other and witness outside the group. Community will be built as members give sacrificially in love to each other. Then the cell must multiply as it grows too large. These are principles which apply to any denomination.

As we continued to consider the cell-group model, I was also struck by how it fitted with my favoured approach to evangelism. I have always felt a passion to seek the lost. I could not be content with getting on with 'church life' even though I saw the importance of the Christian community. I have always been aware of those around who do not know Jesus, and who do not see God as being knowable or relevant. I am not an evangelist, but I do evangelise. I had always found the aggressive approach to evangelism such as street preaching and door knocking rather daunting. I had embraced a belief in 'friendship evangelism' which concentrated on the need for relationship between those who were witnessing and those who were witnessed to.

Many years earlier I had been struck by the writings of Jim Peterson in the book *Evangelism as a Lifestyle*. He argued in his chapter 'The Puzzling Epistles' how Paul rarely encouraged or exhorted his readers to evangelise.

Paul took it for granted that people were living within relationships and were continually witnessing for Christ as they lived out their faith. This now seemed so relevant to what we were learning of cell-group church strategy. Again I could see that this spoke to churches of all denominations.

Getting agreement

As we moved from the summer to the autumn of 1992, I gradually shared this new vision of the cell-group church with the eldership. It was vital to see whether others in the eldership would also be excited by the vision and could see it working for St John's. It was important that it was not just *my* idea, but also God's will for us. As several elders had been within the church for many years, they were likely to have more insight into the possibility of God's calling us to build on the past in this particular way. We met a number of times to seek God for his guidance, and to discuss together how the actual life of St John's would change week by week. We were now planning to have our evangelistic thrust through mid week groups, not through an open meeting on a Sunday. The Sunday meeting would be primarily to worship God and to equip the Christians, and not evangelistic in nature.

It is a matter of record that the whole of the eldership *did* believe we should proceed down this path of transitioning St John's into a cell-group church. This, however, was just the first step. We now needed to take the vision to our existing group leaders. They were in touch with the people. Before this could ever work, the majority of the congregation had to believe that God was calling us to this. They needed to be excited enough to be involved in making the change.

In late November 1992, the leaders had a weekend away. We explained the vision for a cell-group church and opened the discussion up for all the questions that could be thought of. The enthusiasm that was shown during this weekend surprised me. In fact, by Saturday evening the leadership insisted that we take a secret ballot to decide whether we should pursue this matter further. That had not been the intention of the eldership, as we had no plans beyond bringing the vision to the group leaders for their views. Again, it is a matter of record that the leaders voted unanimously for us to pursue this idea of the cell-group church further. However, some of the leaders said that while they believed God was calling us to become a cell-group church, if it happened they did not want to be cell-group leaders! This showed an early appreciation of the commitment and work that would be involved, even though they had had little time to study the subject in depth. God, I believe, gave this insight to many of the leaders at this time. The truth has obviously been borne out over the years.

The only ones in Europe?

What happened next surprised us all. From contacts in America we heard of the 'International Cell Church Conference' to be held at Faith Community Baptist Church in Singapore at the end of February 1993. Some of our church members were keen to go and to get as much information about the cell-group church as possible before we took the matter further. So five of us went: three of the eldership and two group leaders. Each paid for their own travel, accommodation and the conference fee.

This was a mighty step for any member of St John's. Living in a parish in a relatively poor part of Bradford, few people had money saved up and few were used to going abroad even on holiday. We were only just used to going as delegates to conferences in this country.

Never before had we even considered going abroad to a conference, let alone one on the other side of the world. God wonderfully provided for us. One obtained extra work, another inherited some money and I received a large unexpected gift from a relative. We got there and felt great excitement to be among the 1,000 or so delegates from all over the world.

We were nevertheless shocked to discover that we were the only people from western Europe. There were delegates from every other continent, from such places as Russia and China, many parts of Africa, New Zealand, and both North and South America. Many spoke to us of their burden for western Europe, and how they had been praying for this move of the Holy Spirit across the world also to become evident in western Europe. This was slightly overwhelming, and very exciting.

There was plenty of practical teaching at the conference, and we were also able to see how the cell-group church in Singapore worked in practice. However, the most influential experience for each of us was our respective visits to cell-group meetings. It was obvious that the members were really sharing their lives together, and willing to be open with each other so that God could freely move among them. They worshipped in a simple way and proceeded to pray God's word into each other's lives. They took the pastor's message from the previous Sunday and discussed how it was relevant to their everyday lives. The subject was the Fatherhood of God and I particularly remember prayer for one group member who had been ill-treated by his father in childhood. I believe this man was significantly changed by God during that evening as some of the hurt in his life was healed.

We saw nothing at the conference that dissuaded us from proceeding, and much to excite and encourage us. Ironically for me, it was visiting this church in Singapore that convinced me that the cell-group church structure was not just for churches in the Far Eastern culture. Maybe our structure would never be as regimented as that at Faith Community Baptist Church, but it did become clear to me that God was calling us to be much more efficient and effective in our Church life in Britain. We were being called to greater accountability and responsibility. We were being called to expect God's healing among us in a greater measure. We were being asked to witness for Jesus as a whole church membership in our respective communities. There was a zeal about the Christians in Singapore and the delegates from other parts of the world that we wished we had. We saw God calling us to awaken that zeal in Christians here to love God more, to love each other and to love the lost.

Grasping the nettle

When we returned, we arranged meetings for all the members of the church to consider the way forward. The vision of the cell-group church was put to the church on two occasions so that every member could attend. Once the vision had been explained, the church members were then asked to discuss the way forward in their existing house groups. This happened over the next month, and then we met together again to see what we believed God had been saying. There was plenty of time to disagree, or to ask questions, or to advocate other ways forward. The majority came back either with an enthusiasm to move ahead in this way or with a sense that God was calling us to this path but hesitant because of the certain knowledge of some of the pain it would involve. At this early stage some already understood the greater commitment to which God was calling us.

As we approached the summer of 1993, we agreed that

we would disband all the existing house groups. For some time we had been asking God whether the existing house groups could be changed into cell groups. In the end we felt that many had reached their 'sell-by date'. There would be relief for some members in that they could start afresh in a new cell group. For others it was a time of great sadness because relationships had developed in their fellowship groups that were deep and precious. It is a testimony to many of the members of St John's that they were willing to sacrifice the continuation of these groups for the sake of a clean break from the past, and a new beginning.

The leaders also were given the option to take on the role of leader for the new cell groups. Some did not but the majority did. Over the summer period we held many training sessions for the leaders and apprentice leaders. Looking back, we should have stressed further the difference between being a cell-group leader and a fellowship-group leader. Only some years down the path have we found that it is so easy to revert to being a leader of a group that is still mainly inward looking. The group had to be outward looking from the first meeting.

Ralph Neighbour now states that at its first ever meeting a cell group should make a faith statement as to when it will multiply. That faith statement, including a date, can be continually referred to over the weeks and months that follow. We did not do this, mainly because we felt that the groups would multiply within a short period of time. With hindsight, we can see that in Britain's spiritual culture the multiplication period is probably in the region of eighteen months to two years for the normal cell group. At about the eighteen-month period, one can see whether the group will ever multiply or whether in some way it needs to be reconstituted. These things we have learnt since, but in 1993 we started off in great ignorance.

The groups were finally launched in October 1993. We

began with twelve adult groups, two youth groups, three for those aged between nine and thirteen, two for those aged between five and nine, and one for under-fives. The question we had to answer immediately was how to organise the groups. The church members were aware that the eldership was trying to form these groups, and we began to hear comments from some people as to whom they wanted to be with and more usually whom they definitely did not want to be with! This was a time of insecurity for a number of people and we tried to alleviate this by jokingly suggesting that a notice-board be put up at the back of the church so that people could write down the names of their friends and enemies! This brought home to many the un-Christlike attitudes we so often have concerning others in the church fellowship. It also served as a stark reminder that certain relationships would have to be restored very soon if a group was to be effective.

It had taken fifteen months to launch St John's as a cell-group church from the time when the book had first landed on our doormat. This may seem a long time, but it was necessary for the membership of the church to own the vision. That year and a bit flew by as we tried to get to grips with the change in our thinking about church. Looking back, I can see that change has only really come about as we have worked out cell-group life in practice. We had looked round the country for other examples of cell church to help us, but we were continually disappointed. Churches who were said to have cells had in fact got house groups similar to our old fellowship groups.

We began in naivety and ignorance, but God in his mercy led us to a successful launch. When God gives his vision to a church I believe he honours the steps of obedience that are taken along the way. For us, those steps were big. One of them was learning to build deeper relationships.

CHAPTER 3

BUILDING RELATIONSHIPS

The crucial question is, how well do we really know each other? Perhaps we know so many people that we no longer know who we know! Can I say I know Bill Clinton? I certainly know a lot about him through information fed to me by the media. Now that I have seen him twenty yards away in a car speeding off down a street in New York, can I say I know him better? It is more accurate to say that I am acquainted with him.

Michael Schluter and David Lee, in the concluding chapter of *The R Factor*, argue for the rediscovery of close relationships in society. They say:

In the West, we find ourselves scattered too far and moving too fast to maintain a strong base of counter relationships. Relationship is less and less a matter of sharing the same patch of earth and the same block of air. We meet many more people, but less frequently. We still have friends and families, but on the whole these relationships are fewer, more intermittent, less stable. Instead we feel millions of tiny threads tying us into general and indirect relationship with people we never touch or talk to, people who as individuals we know nothing about nor ever will. This has a profound effect on the way we live. It means that in the mega community we live among strangers.[5]

We can be in situations of close physical intimacy with people and still ignore each other, as anyone who has travelled on the London Underground will have noticed. In fact we often go to great trouble to avoid touching others, such as pausing at doorways or calculating yards in advance which side we are going to pass on a narrow pavement. We are programmed to apologise if we slip up and invade someone else's personal space.

Yet relationships are fundamental to our human life. The first reason for this is that they cannot be avoided. In the normal way of things nearly everything is done in the context of relationships. Most work with or for others. When we eat we usually eat what others have made. When we read, we are reading the words that others have written. The second reason is that not only do we live in relationships, we live for them. Most of us value our relationships above all else. If you ask people what they value most highly, most will speak of those close to them, their loved ones. They may be children, partner or parents. It is rare to hear someone say 'my CD collection' or even 'my car', and when they do we regard them as 'odd'.

The closer our relationship with someone, the more it affects our behaviour. Those involved in business will know that if you are a one-off client of mine and I may never see you again, I may be more strongly tempted to rip you off. If on the other hand I am aware that our dealing is going to continue over a number of years, I am much more likely to behave honourably towards you. As relationships have become more tenuous, the ties which hold society together have been broken.

Relationships in the Bible

The Bible clearly teaches the importance of strong relationships. As society has strayed from its Christian base, relationships have become more superficial. This has also coincided with the advance of new technology that provides us with all manner of information but does little to challenge our values in life.

What then is the biblical pattern of relationships? The first reference to the creation of man by God is made in the context of the trinitarian relationship: 'Let *us* make man in *our* image, in *our* likeness' (Genesis 1:26, my italics). The closeness of relationship in the Trinity is further illustrated when Jesus, the Son of God, is on earth. Even before Jesus' birth, the angel Gabriel makes it clear that the other members of the Trinity, the Father and the Holy Spirit, are intimately involved in the birth of the Son of God (Luke 1:26–37).

Then Jesus himself, even at the age of twelve, shows surprise that his mother would not know he was in his Father's house, the Temple (Luke 2:49). As he begins his ministry, that intimate relationship with the Spirit is clearly shown (Luke 4). Jesus has already heard his Father speak to him at his baptism: 'You are my Son, whom I love; with you I am well pleased' (Luke 3:22). It was a powerful message to Jesus, but it is also one to us as we see the Father speak to him even before his ministry achievements, telling him of his fatherly love for him.

We see the true nature of the incarnation as we continue to read through the Gospels. Jesus always works at the instigation of the Holy Spirit and by his power. We observe Jesus seeing what the Father was doing and then getting involved. He says, 'I tell you the truth, the Son can do nothing by himself; he can do only what he sees his Father doing, because whatever the Father does the Son also does. For the Father loves the Son and shows him all he does. Yes, to your amazement he will show him even greater things than these' (John 5:19–20). Here is the Son of God who has given up the divine attributes of omnipresence to become a man in a particular time and place. He has also given up his omniscience to receive wisdom and knowledge and direction from the Spirit. He has also given up his omnipotence, working instead by the power of the Spirit while he is in human form. The intimate relationship within the Trinity continues.

I wonder whether we have even begun to understand what it meant for Jesus to be 'full of joy through the Holy Spirit' (Luke 10:21), or indeed 'being in anguish'. The *disciples* were exhausted from sorrow, not Jesus (Luke 22:44-45) as he approached the ordeal of the cross. It is only in the context of the trinitarian relationship that we begin to understand these emotions being displayed by Jesus. Likewise, we see the intense pain of Jesus when he cries, 'My God, my God, why have you forsaken me?' (Mark 15:34) as he begins to sense his separation from his Father as he takes the weight of our sin on himself.

I believe this example of deep divine relationship is there to speak to us about our human relationships. The Genesis creation account quickly moves to the statement by God that 'it is not good for the man to be alone. I will make a helper suitable for him' (Genesis 2:18). Human relationships then began. But then came the fall which, though primarily affecting and spoiling our relationship with God our maker, also marred our human relationship with each other. In simple terms the Bible can be said to show how God goes about that long painful process of restoring his relationship with a fallen humanity. But the Bible also shows the continuing struggle to restore right relationships between one human and another. Christianity is a relational religion, not an individualistic one.

In the incarnation we see Jesus as Emmanuel, God with us. He performs miracles, he teaches, but primarily he forms relationships. He seeks out the twelve and makes them his friends: 'I no longer call you servants, because a servant does not know his master's business. Instead, I have called you friends, for everything that I learned from my Father I have made known to you. You did not choose me, but I chose you and appointed you to go and bear fruit—fruit that will last' (John 15:14–16). Jesus lived with his disciples and shared his life with them. They lived in community, dependent upon each other. He was a model of how to be a servant so they could be servants to each other. He showed he loved them so that they could love each other. 'My command is this: Love each other as I have loved you' (John 15:12). He remonstrated with them as they argued among themselves as to who was the greatest. He showed them that this example of loving each other would be a powerful witness to their and every society: 'A new command I give you: Love one another. As I have loved you so you must love one another. By this all men will know that you are my disciples, if you love one another' (John 13:34–35).

Jesus sends out the disciples to witness in pairs. When the disciples take up the mantle of the great commission, they invariably go as teams. We see Peter and John together in Acts 3 and 4 where the crippled beggar is healed and they are brought before the Sanhedrin to explain their actions. Later we see Paul and Barnabas, or Paul with Luke, or Barnabas with Mark. Then there is Paul and Silas, and Paul's association with Timothy.

The great theme of the restoration of relationships continues in Paul's letters and the other epistles. Of course, the emphasis is on the restoration of our relationship with God through the death of Christ and the filling of the Holy Spirit for our daily walk with God. Yet much of it also relates to the restoration of our relationships with one another. As Jesus built relationships with those he met and their lives changed as a result, so it happens with us. Jesus' meeting with Zacchaeus is a good example of this. Zacchaeus first looked on Jesus from afar but at Jesus' instigation the relationship was deepened. They ate and talked together, and through that experience Zacchaeus became a changed man. He was changed to such an extent that it even affected his bank balance as those he had previously swindled were now reimbursed fourfold (Luke 19:1–10)!

Against this background, our Church life must show that we are obeying the commands of Jesus to love one another, and reflecting the example displayed by him in his life on earth and his relationship within the Trinity. Rather than the Church reflecting the superficiality of relationships in society, it must restore the biblical emphasis on depth of relationship. This, I believe, can be done through the development of cell groups within the Church. The Reverend John Cole, the Church of England's Mission Development Advisor, commented on this as he reviewed a recent consultation asking: 'What sort of a church are we called to be?' He states in his subsequent report on the consultation: 'The overwhelming conclusion (and it *felt* overwhelming!) was that from every direction God was leading people to experience "church" no longer primarily through their involvement in a church congregation, but through something more intimate (the cell, the small faith community) and something much richer (the celebration, the communion of communities).'

Deepening relationships in the cell

At St John's we had a crash course in moving to deeper relationships. In the late 1980s a number of people who were recovering alcoholics joined the fellowship. They had been influenced by the Alcoholics Anonymous twelve-step programme, part of which was to be 'rigorously honest'. The effect they had was dramatic. When asked, 'How are you?' many proceeded to explain in detail exactly how they were. Few followed our British convention of saying, 'I'm fine,' regardless of the truth! When they then asked others from the congregation how they were and were met with the stock answer of, 'I'm fine,' they were questioning to say the least. They cross-examined people to find out whether that was really the truth. This was initially most unsettling for the membership of St John's. However, we can now see what a liberating experience this was. Our relationships have become more real as people have gradually gained the confidence to speak of what they are facing in their lives, how they are coping and how they are feeling. Only as David shared with Jonathan about the difficulties of his relationship with Jonathan's father did their relationship move to a deeper level (1 Samuel 20:1).

Membership of a cell group provides an environment for deepening friendships and relationships. This can be illustrated both from what takes place in an individual cell-group meeting and also through the life of the cell group over a period of time. The graph (Figure 4) is based on one given by Ralph Neighbour in *Where Do We Go From Here?* and shows how vital it is to have the different components of the cell-group meeting working well. Only then are the relationships of those within the group deepened.

The axis on the left gives a scale of friendship and relationship. People have been living independently until they come into the meeting, then during the ice-breaker they begin to relate together and to move towards the comfort level of relaxing in each other's presence. This is shown by the line (—). Only when this has been done to some extent can worship 'take off'. This assumes that there is some good worship prepared, and that people find that they are in God's very presence as he comes to

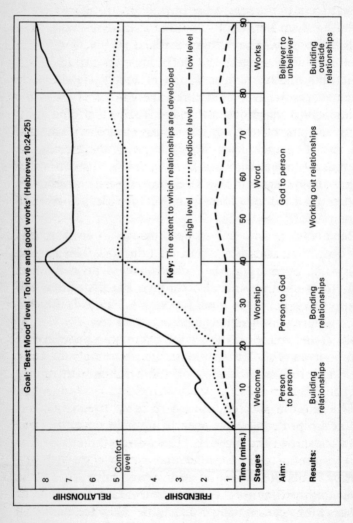

Figure 4. Group life dynamics—micro [6]

dwell in the praises of his people. In other words, they know God is with them at the meeting.

The graph then demonstrates that if that has been the case they are in a much better position to allow God to speak to them through the word and its application. They will feel positive about being changed by him in areas of their lives where necessary. They become open to the possibility that others in the group can be used by God to help them. This often results in different members of the group being prayed for by others for some change that God wants to make in their lives. A church member shared with me that on one particular night at this stage of the meeting he became aware that God was prompting him to tell the other members of the group how he had never really experienced love from his father while growing up. He shared how God had in some measure talked to him during the worship about being a Father to him now and about how he should not be afraid of thinking of God as Father. He would not be let down in the way his earthly father had let him down in the past. Other group members then prayed for him, and from that night his relationship with God the Father has been different, with the barriers removed.

Of course, there are other factors that affect the level of relationship achieved. For instance, how well do these people already know each other? Have they built up any trust in each other? It has been our experience that, whatever level of relationship the group has between members at its inception, this can grow through a successful ice-breaker and well-prepared and executed worship.

The meeting then ends with a bit of 'work'. Members feel good about praying for each other and want to share their faith with others. They may even want now to invite others to the cell meeting in the future. They feel confident in God and are excited by the fact that he goes with them from the meeting.

However, if the meeting has not gone so well the result can be seen from the second line (.....). This line demonstrates what happens when the ice-breaker did not quite take off. The worship actually had been quite well prepared and went well, but the group members were starting from a lower base of relationship. They never quite reached the heights. Perhaps they were rather self-conscious with each other. Perhaps one or two felt left out. What happened then was that when God's word was looked at and the application of it was suggested, only part of what God wanted to do was actually accomplished. Some were more spectators than participants. The overall view as the meeting ended was that they ought to pray for others and ought to look outwards but were not really enthusiastic to do so.

The third line (– – –) shows that the ice-breaker hardly got off the ground and the worship was ill prepared or badly executed. Maybe someone tried to lead the group in song and pitched it at the wrong note. Because people's relationships were fragile, this could not be overcome and the worship went from mediocre to worse. People were not really sure of their God as they came to his word. They were not in a position of faith to receive from God and were not comfortable in each other's presence either. As they drew towards the end of the meeting, some were thinking that they were never going to ask their friends to this cell group. Of course, even though the meeting was fairly disastrous, it's not the end of the world or the end of the group. Yet the cumulative effect upon the relationships of the group could be devastating if this experience was not just an isolated blip.

These long-term effects can be seen from the graph in Figure 5. Again, the graph is based on a similar one by Ralph Neighbour. The original had a time period of 26–29 weeks as this was how long it took for a group in

Singapore to be ready to multiply from one group into two.

The spiritual climate seems to be much cooler in Britain and our experience is that the period it can take for a group to be ready to multiply into two groups can be up to two years. This period is shown in the graph as 104 weeks. This graph takes for granted that the micro graph (Figure 4) works out healthily. In other words, the second graph shows that a group may begin with about six or seven members and then grow continually, reaching an average attendance of twelve after about a year. The group will then come to a peak in membership of thirteen or fourteen and be ready to multiply into two separate groups.

Again, it is vital to see some of the stages of the development of the group. As people get acquainted in the group over a period of weeks, they start to gel together. They begin to get to know and understand each other. Quite often at the end of what some call the 'honeymoon period', there is a conflict period. This is when members of the group suddenly realise they don't really like other members of the group. Can this be overcome? If it can, the group then moves on as a functioning unit, described here as a goal-setting community, that can seek to reach out more effectively. They are in a position to be directed by the Holy Spirit for the future of their group and to move towards multiplication of the group into two.

The goal for our groups is for them to peak at about thirteen or fourteen members. They then multiply. Our experience has been that sometimes a group never gets to this point. Somewhere they have foundered and there is no real future for the group. This is invariably linked to the low level of relationship achieved within the group and the subsequent inability to set goals as a community together.

There is no guarantee that by forming a cell group there

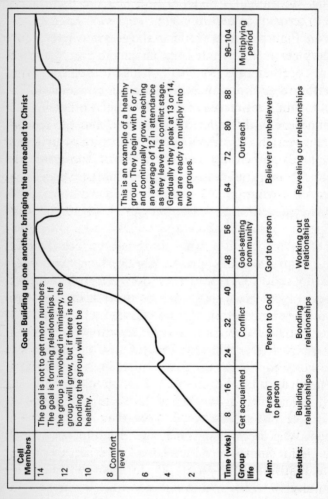

Cell Members	Goal: Building up one another, bringing the unreached to Christ								
14	The goal is not to get more numbers. The goal is forming relationships. If the group is involved in ministry, the group will grow, but if there is no bonding the group will not be healthy.								
12									
10									
8 Comfort level				This is an example of a healthy group. They begin with 6 or 7 and continually grow, reaching an average of 12 in attendance as they leave the conflict stage. Gradually they peak at 13 or 14, and are ready to multiply into two groups.					
6									
4									
2									
Time (wks)	8 16	24 32 40	48 56	64 72 80 88	96–104
Group life	Get acquainted	Conflict	Goal-setting community	Outreach	Multiplying period
Aim:	Person to person	Person to God	God to person	Believer to unbeliever	
Results:	Building relationships	Bonding relationships	Working out relationships	Revealing our relationships	

Figure 5. Group life dynamics—macro

will be a growth in membership and thereby multiplication after a period of time. In Figure 6, the stages in the life of a group are described in some detail. The headings of forming, storming, norming, conforming and performing are another way of describing the stages outlined in the graph in Figure 5. The forming stages are where group members get to know one another in the first weeks of meeting together. The group will then go through a storming period when group members discover personal differences, and this results in conflict with each other. In the norming period, differences are resolved and the fellowship between the members grows. The group members then agree on the purpose and goals of the group as they go through the conforming period. The group then performs in that group members will grow in maturity and use their gifts and the group will grow in numbers of members.

Yet this diagram also shows the dangers which a group faces at each stage of its life. It has been our experience that all groups go through the storming period (the conflict period). Even those groups where members were already friends have still found this to be true. In the group life they are being called to go beyond superficial relationships and that involves a real cost. People annoy each other. People have hurt each other, even in the short time they have known each other. This especially happens in the forming period. People have habits that others don't like. People are insensitive, domineering or just plain talkative. Whatever it is, this is a vital period for the group. Praise God it's not a social club. God is so needed at this time actually to allow people to grow together in community.

It is also vital at this stage to be honest with each other. The group will never get past this stage if the members are not honest. If they refuse to acknowledge that they have a

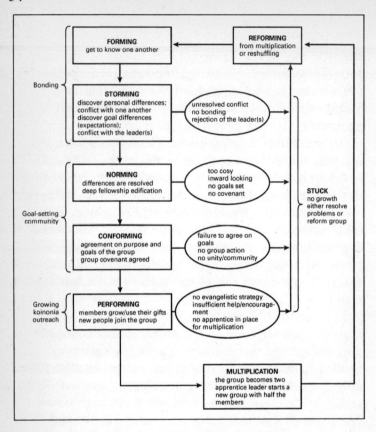

Figure 6. Stages in the life of a group

problem with someone else, or refuse to deal with it, the group is ultimately a dead duck. The role of the leader is vital as he or she leads by example. The leader needs to be 'happy' in the presence of conflict and not run away from it. Quite often our reaction to trouble is 'flight' or 'fight'. Some will naturally want to avoid any conflict and confrontation, whereas others will naturally relish getting stuck into the fight.

However much we like to think the opposite, these

problems will not go away, and for a group to move to a deeper level God needs to come in at this stage to resolve the problems. The leader must seek to resolve any conflict and to encourage group members to face up to their differences. At this stage God does come in to help us forgive others and to repent of our own faults and prejudices.

For example, one of our groups recently set aside a whole evening to tell each other the truth. Although this is not always the best way to resolve conflict, it worked for this group. Everyone finally agreed to say exactly what they thought of the group meeting and, indeed, of the other group members. The leaders did not escape the flak. One person shared how they had felt let down by the other group members when they were ill and could not attend the group for a period. Little care had been shown and no one had visited. Another revealed that they always felt put down by a certain member of the group. They talked of how they were now afraid to voice their opinion as they expected to be made to look foolish.

It was a testimony to God breaking in that the group went from strength to strength after this meeting. Working it out took many weeks and some of it had to be done 'behind the scenes' with ones and twos meeting together to resolve their conflicts.

This is so often missing in Church life, but it is vital to cell group and Church life. In many years' Church experience I have found that Christians are not always willing to deal with their hurts and prejudices, their likes and dislikes. However, isn't this what God is calling us to as his Church? How liberating it is for a church to move to this greater level of honesty and reality. It is restricting to have to be very careful about what you say and do around other people. If you are always afraid that you may touch one of their hurts, or provoke one of their prejudices, it makes for an uneasy relationship. It is like walking on eggshells around some people because either you do not know what their reaction will be, or you are all too aware of their potential reaction. For instance, they are likely to burst into tears or display great anger. These hurts and prejudices need dealing with, and we have found that God uses the cell-group meetings to do so.

This honesty and reality is required in other circumstances, too. For instance, a person in one of our cell groups continually displayed a superior, judgemental attitude to other members of the group. As trust developed in the group through other members sharing their feelings of low self-esteem, this person finally confessed to having the same feelings. It turned out that his superiority complex was in fact an inverted inferiority complex. He felt bad about himself so compensated by trying to put everyone else down.

Having moved through the conflict, storming stage, the group is now much more of a functioning unit where members enjoy deep fellowship and each is used by God to build up the others. If group members are open about their fears and their frailties, then they are in a position to accept encouragement and support from other members of the group. Only recently a middle-aged woman was able to tell of how she was still frightened of the dark and had to sleep with the light on. She had come to the stage where she knew she could trust other members not to make fun of her or belittle the problem. She found that some were able to sympathise and others were even able to empathise. She testified later to being encouraged even before there was any prayer. Later in the meeting, during specific prayer for the problem, God revealed the reasons for the fear and healed her. Each of our cell groups are able to give examples of similar experiences once members have become comfortable enough to share details of their life, what they are really like, and how they really feel.

Then comes the next danger. This is one of being too cosy and inward looking when no goals are set and there is no covenant relationship with one another. The group must set goals or it will become stuck with no growth. The group members are called to conform, that is to agree on the group's purpose and start living out their deeper relationships, not only in the group meeting but throughout the week. They become a living illustration of Jesus' command to love one another.

As the group develops its evangelistic strategy it will grow in number to peak at about thirteen or fourteen as new people join the group. The apprentice leader will then begin a new group with half the original members.

So it can be seen that the growth of the group and thereby the growth of the Church is specifically linked to the building of relationships. As people get acquainted, so their relationship builds. Then, through the resolution of conflict, those relationships are tested out and deepen further. The group members then begin working together with specific shared goals for the group. It follows that others who are close to group members, such as friends, relatives and workmates, notice that there is a level of love, care and support between the group members that contrasts with the superficiality of many relationships in society. As Jesus said, 'Love one another. As I have loved you, so you must love one another. By this all men will know that you are my disciples if you love one another' (John 13:34–35).

Before leaving this subject of relationship, it is necessary to emphasise the cost involved. Not every Christian will find it easy to go to a deeper level in relationship. Many will be fearful to do so and feel an unwillingness to become vulnerable to others. Yet I believe it is a biblical injunction for each of us as followers of Christ. As Jesus calls us to love each other, I believe there is thereby implied a level of vulnerability. Jesus himself demonstrated this by his willingness to become a man and to live among us. We are called to have the same attitude as that of Jesus whose actions are perfectly described in Philippians 2:6–11. We are called to obey and to 'continue to work out [our] salvation with fear and trembling, for it is God's purpose who works in [us] to will and to act according to his good purpose' (Philippians 2:12–13).

CHAPTER 4

LEADERSHIP

'The task of the professional clergy in the Church of the future will not be to provide primary pastoral care. The task of the professional clergy will be to build and support carers and leaders.' So says Carl George in his book *Prepare Your Church for the Future.*[7] This goes against what is taught in most of our theological training colleges for clergy. Ministers leave college and take up their first posts as junior pastors or curates with the belief that they are 'shepherds'—those who provide primary pastoral care. But I believe this is an impossible vision for their role.

A role for the clergy

Most people accept that clergy are to be involved in the pastoral care of their 'flock'. But should it be primary pastoral care? Should they be the ones who are first and foremost to be used by God to meet the needs and heal the hurts of those who belong to the church congregation? Another widely accepted role model for the clergy is that of welcomer and discipler with those who are new contacts. Invariably it is the clergy who run the initiation course, whether it is Alpha, basics, foundations, baptism or confirmation class. Often members of the congregation make appointments with the clergy for their friends who are wanting to find out more about Christianity or wanting to become Christians.

The problem is that the more a congregation grows, the more time is taken up caring for those already in membership. If these are not cared for, they will drift away hurt and disappointed. But if it is the clergy who are giving primary pastoral care, then the time available to spend with new contacts is drastically cut. A recent study by Steve Croft, Principal of Cranmer Hall, Durham, suggests that when church membership exceeds 100, the minister has no time at all to spend with new contacts (see Figure 7).[8]

At least five common methods have been used to try and raise this ceiling. The first is to work harder, faster and longer. In fact, this is the most common solution and many clergy will evaluate their job satisfaction by how exhausted they are each Saturday evening. This, however, is no solution as it leads to burnout. The second is to reduce the congregation's expectations of quality care. This then defeats the object because the church will not grow. Church growth consultants say churches get bigger by getting better at caring, not by thinning it out.

The third method is to take on another full-time pastor. In many churches this is not possible, either because there are no clergy available or because of money constraints. However, this can raise the ceiling and be a real help. But is it the real solution? The fourth method is to take time from other activities. For example, a church can employ an administrator and delegate some of the tasks previously done by the minister. It certainly follows the biblical precedent of Acts 6 where seven men were appointed to oversee the daily distribution of food. The twelve apostles were then able to give their attention to prayer and the ministry of the word

Suppose a minister has 10 hours per week for primary pastoral care. See how this changes as the church grows:

Size of church	Hours with new contacts	Hours with existing church members
30	7	3
60	4	6
90	1	9
120		12
150		15

Even at its best, this allows for approximately one hour every quarter with each person. The size of a 'traditional church' congregation will always be limited by the number of pastoral hours available. All churches have a pastoral care ceiling!

Figure 7.

(Acts 6:1–7). Certainly, in this method the ceiling is raised a little but some time is spent in managing tasks done by others.

I believe the real solution comes through allowing the church to be the church! The pastoral care of the congregation should be handed over primarily to the congregation itself. The clergy move from being the people who provide care to being the people who ensure care is provided. I believe Acts 6 is in fact the first step in this delegation of pastoral care to members of the church. Hence from recognising a real problem experienced by many clergy today we see a pointer towards the style of

leadership employed in the cell-group church. I shall look
further at this a little later.

The dynamics of the congregation

It is necessary first to understand the dynamics of a
Christian congregation and how they change according
to the size and structure of the congregation.

First there is 'the family church' which has between one
and fifty members. A church of this size is usually
dominated by a few human 'dynasties'. Certain families
are very important to the running of the church and are
involved in most activities of that church. The minister is
in effect a chaplain to the congregation.

Secondly, there is the pastoral church. This has between
50 and 150 members with approximately 100 adults. Here
the minister pastors everyone and there are indeed high
expectations of personal pastoral care. The church can
grow until it reaches a pastoral care ceiling as described
above.

Thirdly, there is the programme church. Here the
church has between 150 and 400 members and there are
many lay-led programmes. There are men's meetings and
women's meetings, youth activities and clubs, ministries
among singles and the divorced, central prayer meetings,
Bible studies and the like. These groupings, however, do
not usually provide much primary pastoral care. It can be
increased, perhaps by the employment of further pastors,
but these are usually also involved in resourcing the programmes that are in existence. The programme church
also appears to reach a ceiling. The church may come to
feel more and more like a large organisation or corpora-
tion. A higher and higher proportion of the members will
not be or feel involved. Twenty per cent of the congregation may well be running programmes for the other eighty
per cent who attend.

Then there is the cell-group church. Here there can be anything between two members and a million members. The pastoral care is devolved to the groups and so is the mission. As the cell groups come together they can meet in single or multiple congregations. Here the minister teaches and resources the church to bring about effective pastoral care and mission. The emphasis is then on church life taking place around the homes of members rather than from a central location.

This idea of regrouping church life around the home has been common down the centuries. From the birth of the Christian movement, as recorded by Luke, the first believers met day by day not only in the Temple, which was the gathering of the whole congregation, but also in their homes, '[eating] together with glad and sincere hearts, praising God and enjoying the favour of all the people' (Acts 2:46–47; 20:6–11; Hebrews 10:23–25).

The New Testament records on many occasions that Christians met in homes. Of course, Christians did meet in the synagogues and also on occasion, it would appear, in hired halls (see Acts 19:9). The upper room at Troas (Acts 20:7ff) may well also have been quite a large room. However, such references are far outweighed by those relating to people's houses or homes. There was Jason's house at Thessalonica, Titus Justus' house situated provocatively opposite the synagogue at Corinth, Philip's house at Caesarea and Lydia's house at Philippi. Aquila and Priscilla seemed to have maintained a church in their home wherever they lived, in Corinth, Rome and Ephesus. The jailer's house at Philippi was used as an evangelistic centre after his dramatic conversion. Stephanas' household was baptised by Paul in person and Paul apparently used his home 'for the service of the saints'. The upper room of the house owned by the mother of Mark in Jerusalem was the earliest known meeting place of the Church. Therefore it is hardly surprising that the church in the house became a crucial factor in the spread of the Christian faith. Further references to the New Testament Church meeting in a home setting can be found in 1 Corinthians 16:19, Romans 16:5, Colossians 4:15, Acts 5:42.

Consequently, two of the major emphases of the Church, namely pastoral care and mission, are maintained from a small cell-group setting.

The adoption of a new leadership structure

So what does this mean for the clergy? What has this meant for me and my role in the Church? Prior to beginning our path of transition to a cell-group church, our membership was in the lower numbers of a programme church, at about 150 adults and children. We had tried to widen the pastoral care net by appointing another pastor but still found that twenty per cent of members were running programmes for the other eighty per cent. Hence the frustration I described in chapter 2. We had already taken some steps away from the traditional Anglican Church structure of leadership. An eldership was in place and there were group leaders who were readily seen as the second 'tier' of leadership.

We then adopted the structure shown in Figure 8. Each cell-group leader has a cell-group co-ordinator. That co-ordinator will have up to five leaders under his or her care. He or she is a pastor to the cell-group leader but also gives advice, encouragement, training, trouble-shooting and ministry for healing to the cell-group member alongside the cell-group leader. The cell-group co-ordinator has authority delegated from the leadership of the church and consequently the cell-group leader is accountable to him or her. In turn the cell-group co-ordinator relates to an area pastor whose role is primarily one of support,

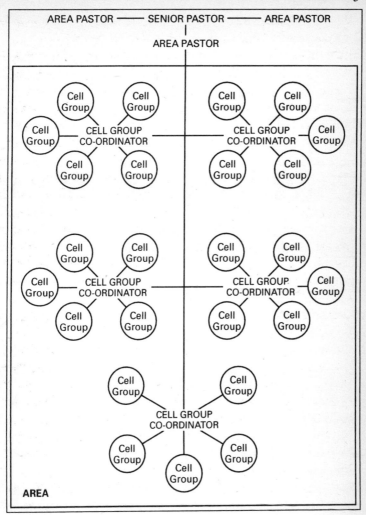

Figure 8. Leadership structure–working model

care and encouragement, but with further elements of training.

In the diagram there are twenty-five cell groups, five cell-group co-ordinators ministering to those leaders, and one area pastor ministering to the needs of the five cell-group co-ordinators. If this 'area' related to our adult work, then we may be talking of something in the region of 250 cell-group members, there being approximately ten in each cell.

Here we can see that there can be other areas with area pastors. For instance, the whole of the youth work may be an area in itself. The pattern would be duplicated for that area. In reality our structure is slightly more complicated in that we have fifteen cells of adults at this time, the leaders of which relate to four cell-group co-ordinators. These co-ordinators relate to me as I take on the role of area pastor. I am also area pastor for the cell group co-ordinator of the youth cell groups (at present six in number), the 9+ years cell groups (six in number), and the 0–9 years cell groups (five in number). I am taking on the role of senior pastor at the present time as well as area pastor.

As we grow, the next level of delegation will have to take place. We will need to appoint area pastors and my role will then be to relate primarily to them. Strictly speaking we should have two cell-group co-ordinators in the youth and in 9+ work, because we already have more than five cells in those areas. No doubt it would work better if there were two cell-group co-ordinators, each relating to three cell-group leaders rather than the present one relating to six. However, the right person is not available to do the job at present.

Always there is the temptation to make do with present imperfect structures rather than to fight for the liberation that can come about through implementing this better structure. Indeed, Ray Macauley, who has had experience with cell churches in New Zealand, now advocates that the ratio of one cell-group co-ordinator to three cell-group leaders is more likely to provide the input required for successful cell-group leading. However, this then introduces the whole problem of finding enough leaders. I find it amazing that already we have roughly one third of our adult membership involved in leading groups. Where have we found them all? Where will we find more? What sort of people are we looking for?

How Jesus trained leaders

Jesus was the most effective developer of leaders that we can find. His leaders were extremely successful in managing to 'turn the world upside down' with a revolution that was spiritual in nature but affected the social, political and economic life of his time. How did Jesus do it?

One of the first keys to this is that he plainly set out his kingdom purpose. It was to make disciples. In many churches there is a major difference between the accepted purpose of the church and the actual purpose of the church. The accepted purpose sometimes appears on a written mission statement which congregational members are encouraged to learn by heart. More often the accepted purpose is rather vague, perhaps involving worship, pastoral care and evangelism. But does this then reflect the actual purpose? The actual purpose is lived out in the daily activities, programmes, buildings and financial statements of the church. Any evaluation of leadership effectiveness must be made in reference to the actual purpose, not the stated one.

Therefore in the cell-group church, where the stated purpose is to make disciples within the context of small groups, that actual purpose must be lived out through its leaders. These leaders must be actively involved in nurturing a cell group, a basic Christian community, so its members become effective ministers and missionaries. If, on the other hand, the majority of church members' energy, time and resources is being used to run Sunday activities then *that* is the actual purpose of the church. As Jesus said in Matthew 6:21—'For where your treasure [time, energy, resources, priorities] is, there your heart will be also.' If this is true, then the leaders best suited to maintain such a purpose will be people with organising and administering gifts.

With the cell-group church we are, I believe, getting back to Jesus' *primary purpose* for his Church, which is to make disciples. We have to find leaders who have that primary purpose on their heart and are willing to be trained in it.

Jesus also knew that a structural 'wineskin' is essential in the development of leaders. There needs to be a framework, a context in which leaders can be trained to fulfil their assigned purpose. A DIY power drill fits well into the context of home improvements but is inappropriate in the hands of a dentist! Church wineskins should be appropriate for containing and preserving the Church's spiritual purposes. So it is, I believe, that many churches with a Sunday programme structure have little success in producing effective New-Testament type leaders.

Jesus set his kingdom purpose of making kingdom disciples within the context of his kingdom structure. It was a kingdom community of small groups through which he lived and worked. Jesus developed his leaders through direct relationship to his presence, his power and his ministry purpose. For three years they lived in community with him and so he was able to make them fishers of men who were also able to feed his sheep.

The same is true now. Leaders can be developed to work

out Jesus' purpose and his promises for his Church. Bill Beckham has produced a list for comparison of Jesus' leadership method with our own leadership approach.[9]

How God looks on leaders

It is helpful to go back before the time of Jesus to see how God chose leaders. In 1 Samuel 16 we find Samuel instructed by God in leadership selection.

> When they arrived, Samuel saw Eliab and thought, 'Surely the Lord's anointed stands here before the Lord.' But the Lord said to Samuel, 'Do not consider his appearance or his height, for I have rejected him. The Lord does not look at the things man looks at. Man looks at the outward appearance, but the Lord looks at the heart.' Then Jesse called Abinadab and made him pass in front of Samuel. But Samuel said, 'The Lord has not chosen this one either.' Jesse then made Shammah pass by, but Samuel said, 'Nor has the Lord chosen this one.' Jesse made seven of his sons pass before Samuel, but Samuel said to him, 'The Lord has not chosen these.' So he asked Jesse, 'Are these all the sons you have?' 'There is still the youngest,' Jesse answered, 'but he is tending the sheep.' Samuel said, 'Send for him; we will not sit down until he arrives.' So he sent and had him brought in. He was ruddy, with a fine appearance and handsome features. Then the Lord said, 'Rise and anoint him; he is the one.'
>
> (1 Samuel 16:6–12)

This passage reminds me of how exasperating the task of finding and training cell-group leaders has often been. I have gone into the process with preconceived notions about what a future leader looks like and have found myself ready to anoint the wrong man or woman. At St John's we have often looked for things like maturity, zeal, knowledge, confidence and a good education. Although

We can compare our leadership approach with Jesus':
• His leadership was simple and focused
• Leaders were reproduced while doing the task
• Outside financial assistance was not required
• Apprenticeship training took place on the job while doing the basic task
• Jesus narrowed the gap between leaders and members
• Leaders could function every day of the week as a lifestyle and not just on 'Sunday'
• Leaders were engaged in life transformation rather than in information
• Small workable units (small groups) encouraged a realistic supervision ratio
• Success was defined in spiritually qualitative terms rather than numerical terms
• The small group provided the context where the task could be accomplished
• The primary vision could be verbalised in a simple statement
• Servanthood, not position and honour, was the motivation of leadershp
• Jesus minimised administration and maximised relationships
• Leaders equipped the saints for the work of ministry, instead of doing all the tasks
The Church of the twentieth century desperately needs Jesus to develop leaders with first-century power.

Figure 9.

none of these is wrong, they are simply of secondary importance. We have discovered through bitter experience that we can have leaders who possess all these traits but who still do not have the anointing from God.

We have therefore learnt to begin where God does, with the heart. We now look for leaders who will prove a 'HIT'. We look for Holiness and humility of heart, for Integrity, and for an attitude of Thankfulness. This does not mean to say that we expect people to be sinless before they can be leaders, but we do look for a desire of the heart to be *holy*. A right view of yourself before God (humility) is vital to the growth in holiness. John Wesley acknowledged that the closer he got to God in his relationship, the more he was aware of his own sin.

Then there is *integrity*. There is a certain openness about a good leader. What you see is what you get. You know where they are coming from and you know you can trust them because they have no hidden agendas. They are not trying to impress you or trying to hide their short-comings. They are willing to be vulnerable to others when necessary, in order to encourage others to be open before God.

It makes such a difference when someone lives out *thankfulness* to God in their lives. It produces a right dependence upon him for the task of leadership. Some of our leaders show clearly the gratitude they have to God for saving them. They see that it is only through God's love and power that they have been able to break free from the downward spiral in their lives. Sometimes it has been drugs or alcohol, or broken and destructive relationships, or maybe just the drudgery and pointless-ness of life. God has changed their lives and they thank him.

What, then, is the place of people's gifts and personal-ity? They are certainly important, but not in comparison with their state of heart. One couple in our church were reluctant to take on leadership as they did not believe they had the gifts. Yet we saw that there were signs of holiness, integrity and thankfulness in them. It has been great to see God use their personalities in this task and to gift them so that they are effective leaders both pastorally and evangelistically. He even gave them confidence to withstand the conflict period within their group so that they are now working towards multiplication of the group within the next months.

The calling and training of new leaders

In fact, the key to having enough leaders is having enough apprentice leaders already in place.

Some time ago, I was panicking about finding enough leaders to take on all our groups. As I prayed about the problem, I felt that God was telling me to stop panicking about leaders and start panicking about not having enough apprentice leaders! We have still some way to go in thinking like this, but we have recently tried to make sure that all our adult groups have an apprentice leader in place at the group's inception.

This makes so much sense as the cell groups attempt to grow and draw in new people. Within the foreseeable future each group will divide into two groups. Therefore there is an urgent need to grow new leaders from the beginning. An apprentice leader in place at the beginning is like a prophetic sign to the group that it will multiply. Where there has not been an apprentice leader in place at the beginning of a group's life, then everyone should understand it is a priority to seek one. We have seen the Lord single out a group member over a period of weeks so that the leader, the person themselves, and other group members have become aware that they are that apprentice leader for the future. Perhaps they take leaps forward in the 'HIT' qualities and become effective in leading other group members in parts of the group meeting.

Jesus trained his leaders by apprenticeship. Throughout the Gospels there is a learning process taking place for the disciples (eg Mark 3:13–19; 6:6–13). We also see it in the Acts of the Apostles, with Barnabas and Saul (Acts 9:27; 13:1–3; 14:1). Then there is Paul in Ephesus (Acts 20:30–38) and Paul's advice to Timothy: 'You then, my son, be strong in the grace that is in Christ Jesus. And the things you have heard me say in the presence of many witnesses entrust to reliable men who will also be qualified to teach others' (2 Timothy 2:12). Indeed, as we scan the pages of the New Testament, there is no other model of leadership training. The disciples caught the vision of Jesus' purpose and started living it out.

The development of an apprentice leader primarily takes place on the job. Every person and partnership will be different. The way things develop and the speed of development will need to be discussed between the cell-group leader, the apprentice leader, and the cell-group co-ordinator. It is important not to rush things, as good leaders do take time to grow. For some it will be months but for others it can be a year.

The training includes three key elements. The first is prayer, through which we acknowledge and depend on God for the development of the group. The apprentice leader will meet regularly with the leader to pray for the group members and also for the group meetings. Through experience of seeing God answer prayer the apprentice leader's own prayer life will be encouraged and his or her faith will be increased. Sometimes records are kept of the prayers that have been prayed for specific people or for certain events so that the answers can be readily seen.

Secondly, there is the development of skill and vision.

This happens when potential leaders read books, listen to tapes and go to training courses. Later they also go to the leadership meetings with the cell-group co-ordinator and the area pastors. The wider vision of the cell-group church and the more detailed vision for the growth of the cell group will be explained in detail during this time, with opportunities for questions and discussion. Specific skills relating to leading meetings, caring and ministering to people will be passed on.

Thirdly, the apprentice is delegated tasks. This is hands-on training, so experience must be obtained in practical ways. In time the apprentice leader may ensure new Christians are nurtured, or organise the group's outreach, or lead the discussion about biblical application.

Following these elements of training, the cell-group leader and the apprentice leader must reflect on them together. We learn as we get good feedback on what has gone well and on what hasn't. This takes time. It is called experience. The story is told of a successful company chairman who was retiring. His successor visited him and asked if he had any advice to give. 'Just two words I have for you—right decisions.' The younger man thought a bit and asked, 'But how do I make right decisions?' 'Just one word,' said the chairman, 'experience.' The younger man said, 'But how do I get that?' The older man looked at him and said, 'Just two words I have for you—wrong decisions.' We all need time to learn, and we learn from our mistakes. But there does come a time when the cell-group leader stands back and hands the reins over to the apprentice leader. This usually happens in the later periods of a group's life before it multiplies. In effect the leader has a sabbatical period of about three months before taking up the leadership reins again with half of the original group.

Ongoing support for the leaders

The cell-group leaders are key people in the cell-group church. The health of the church is reflected in the spiritual health of its cell-group leaders. We rarely see a healthy cell group with a struggling leader. Consequently, the cell-group leader needs regular support and spiritual sustenance.

The cell-group leader's role, with its elements of pastoring, managing and leading, is not easy. It is the specific calling of the cell-group leader to shepherd and pastor in such a way that relationships between group members are built up. The leader has to care for the members and be willing to pray for healing for some of them over a period of time. He or she also has the responsibility of drawing newcomers into the cell group, as well as equipping the next apprentice leader.

As a manager, the cell-group leader needs to see that the machinery of running the cell is in place and actually empowers members to grow in their relationship with the Lord. So the leader will plan and execute the goals of the group. He or she will monitor it and report back to the co-ordinator at each stage of a cell group's life. There is also a need to see how each new Christian is developing in their walk with the Lord, and how they are relating to other members. Some new Christians may well have particular issues to be dealt with or questions to be answered. For instance, a leader was telling me recently of a new member of their group who has now certainly come out of the 'honeymoon period'. It seems he could not stop grinning for the first month of being a Christian. However, these feelings of happiness have been replaced by an awareness of how God is wanting to deal with the pain he feels relating to the separation from his wife some years back. The whole question of loneliness is on the agenda, too. The leader has to be alongside such a new Christian, or at least make sure that someone else of some maturity in the group is there to help and support.

Then the leader leads. The leader must rally the members of the cell group to the purpose and goal. It is vital to continue to promote and communicate these regularly, to pass on any new instructions coming from the whole church leadership. The leader must head up the outreach. For example, one leader made a study of the geographical area in which the cell group met. He then led them in a walk round the area praying for the inhabitants of the houses, the businesses and other key locations such as the post office where people meet regularly. The leader gives a clear lead in attending prayer meetings, demonstrating the necessity of dependence on God for group growth.

One of the key principles we have seen is that a cell-group leader needs a small, clearly defined area of responsibility, low initial training and a high level of ongoing support. This is in marked contrast to most approaches to ministry in the Church, as I and many clergy have experienced over the years. We have been given an impossibly large area of care. We are expected to care for too many people and then told it is not enough just to care for them; we also have to go and reach outsiders and care for them too. We have been given high initial training, such as in theological college or as an assistant minister or curate, but then little or no pro-active ongoing support. We have, in effect, been told that we should only contact those 'above us' if we have a problem. In my Anglican situation, it is implied that things must be pretty desperate before I should seek out the archdeacon or the bishop for help. Ongoing contact is so minimal that, should I be contacted by either the archdeacon or the bishop I immediately wonder what I have done wrong! This is not their fault, but the fault of the system which requires them in turn to care for too many people.

These key principles of a concentrated span of care, low initial training and high ongoing input are therefore vital for our cell-group leaders to feel comfortable, supported and envisioned. This can only be done when we adopt the cell structure and then make sure that those in leadership meet together on a regular basis.

Since beginning cell groups, we have adopted a pattern for leadership meetings which Carl George outlined in his writings. He described them as 'VHS' meetings (meaning that they should consist of three equal elements: Vision— to keep on stating the vision to the leaders; Huddle—a chance for leaders to get together to go through problems and to receive prayer; and Skills—a time of training on a particular aspect of leading). We have adapted the name of the meetings to the more British title of 'VAT' (Vision, Appreciation/Affirmation, Training).

We have these meetings every month. After a short time of worship to put aside our thoughts on the activities of the day and concentrate on God, I spend about twenty minutes or so reminding the leaders of their vital part in the overall work and mission of the church. Sometimes I can give details of what is happening across the world, or maybe in our nation or our city. At times I have reiterated some of the basic cell-church principles relating to the effective care of each other within the group and the effective evangelistic outreach from the group. Alternatively, I may take a biblical truth or promise and expound it with a view to building up the leaders' faith.

The appreciation/affirmation part of the meeting is vital so that the leaders can share with each other some of their experiences and receive prayer for situations that they face and for which they sometimes feel inadequate. Sometimes we have asked our leaders to share in a group with three or four others what has recently encouraged them about life in their particular group, and one aspect with which they are presently struggling. A leader may share an encouraging story about a particular member who has become a Christian and then go on to tell of how she is frustrated by the one group member who shows no sign of growing spiritually at all. In fact, the member has been a negative influence on the group for a few months now and gives every indication of not wanting to change their outlook. The leader would then no doubt receive prayer for wisdom.

In the training time, a particular subject will be chosen so the leaders feel more equipped to lead in the future. We have at times looked at questions of ministering to the bereaved, how to be more effective in praying for the sick, how to get the group praying out loud in group meetings, how to use apprentice leaders effectively, and such like.

Conclusion

Only with an effective support mechanism can we expect our cell-group leaders to flourish and grow in their role. After four years of experience we still know that we have the right leadership structure and are fairly confident that we have the right theories of leadership support and training. We just need to perfect that theory in practice. It is painful for me to see leaders who have lost their vision or who are spiritually burnt out simply because we have not been diligent or experienced enough as church leaders to provide all they needed at this time. I take responsibility for this because, as Carl George says, 'The task of the professional clergy will be to build and support carers and leaders.'

My role has certainly changed since we took the step of becoming a cell-group church in 1993. The most obvious change is that I see less of the ordinary membership of the church to give advice or to pray with them. It has been a conscious decision to encourage the members of the church to see their group leader in the first instance and, even if they need prayer over a period of time for a particular illness or problem, I would encourage this to be with their cell-group leader and, if necessary, the cell-group co-ordinator. Of course, I do still see people, and part of my role now is to train some of the leaders in how to pray effectively with their group members. This is not always easy to organise, but I do try to make sure that if I feel it right to pray with a group member at least the cell-group leader is alongside me to learn and to give their own input and expertise as well.

My main pastoral role is with the leadership of the church. I believe I should spend more time with the 'well' of the church rather than the 'ill' of the church. By this I believe I should encourage and develop the faith of those who are committed to God and seeking to grow in maturity as Christians, ie the leadership and potential future leadership. Looking back, I know that I used to spend much more time with those who 'had a problem' than with those who did not. I do, of course, still see some who 'have a problem', but it is usually the more extreme cases.

Much of my time is also spent in preparation of material for training and also weekly sermons. God challenged me to use my gift of preaching more effectively so that his word could be easily applied within the groups.

The most challenging change to my role has been the awareness that God would have me spend more time with him in prayer. This is so that I can receive direction from him for the church as a whole but also specifically in intercession for the group leaders and members. I do not consider myself to be an intercessor, but I do know that God has called me to this extra commitment in prayer. This has been very challenging to me because I am an active person who wants to be out and doing things, rather than taking the more passive role of listening to God first.

Consequently, a typical week in my life may now consist of a day's preparation work, a day getting away to hear from God and doing some study, a day when I meet with other staff members and other ministers in the area, and a couple of days to see leaders and co-ordinators, and do more preparation. That then leaves my day off and, of course, Sunday with its services. I hope this reflects adequate 'support for carers and leaders' within the church.

CHAPTER 5

EQUIPPING EVERY MEMBER

It is every pastor's dream that each member of his or her congregation should be a fully functioning member of the body of Christ. No longer should it be twenty per cent who are 'going for it' watched by eighty per cent in the pews, but instead every member can be mobilised, when they are fully trained.

The description in Ephesians 4 of the body of Christ is well known, but it needs re-emphasising for the Church in our times, especially here in Britain.

It was he [Christ] who gave some to be apostles, some to be prophets, some to be evangelists, and some to be pastors and teachers, to prepare God's people for works of service, so that the body of Christ may be built up until we all reach unity in the faith and in the knowledge of the Son of God and become mature, attaining to the whole measure of the fulness of Christ. Then we will no longer be infants, tossed back and forth by the waves, and blown here and there by every wind of teaching and by the cunning and craftiness of men in their deceitful scheming. Instead, speaking the truth in love, we will in all things grow up into him who is the Head, that is, Christ. From him the whole body, joined and held together by every supporting ligament, grows and builds itself up in love, as each part does its work.

(Ephesians 4:11–16)

As we have taken steps to beome a cell-group church, part of the process has been to prepare God's people here at St John's for 'works of service'. We have sought to bring members to maturity so that they can focus on whatever God has called them to do in the battle. In some ways it just happened to be a methodical process but with hindsight I believe it has needed to be. The key themes from this passage in Ephesians are unity, maturity, stability, honesty, support, growth and service. Although someone may well develop like this over a period of time, we have tried to accelerate the process. In other words, we have tried to provide a 'fast track' for equipping our saints.

We first heard of such an equipping process when we visited Faith Community Baptist Church in Singapore. There, new members entered a training programme that was called 'a year of equipping' and we have modelled our training programme on this to some extent. This means that someone who joins our church today will be trained in the themes of Ephesians 4 far more quickly than they would have before we became a cell-group church. Obviously such a training programme can exist in churches that are not cell-group churches. It is, however, an essential part of the life of cell-group churches. Every member has the opportunity of being trained and equipped to minister both within the body of the church and outside.

In our situation, as we changed into a cell-group church in 1993, we found that our previous training of members had been patchy. Most had been through the Foundations Course (a bit like Alpha) but then only the keener Christians would go on to further training. For instance, some would undertake a training course and then join the evangelism team. Some had joined ministry teams who prayed with people for healing. Some had felt called to become intercessors and received further training for this. Many people went to conferences outside the church, but no detailed records were kept as to who had done what course, with whom and when. As a leadership we saw the need to 'get our act together' and become more methodical and purposeful in training the church.

I believe it was when we started taking seriously the fact that Christians are involved in a war that we saw the need for some basic training. Minds needed to be disciplined and skills needed to be honed. We longed for a church which had people who could train others in these areas because they had already done it themselves. It comes back to the necessity for church members to be disciples and to then be ready to also disciple others (2 Timothy 2:2).

Travel guide for disciples

We began by developing a 'Journey Guide'. This is a short booklet for each member to read and fill out to enable them to answer the question 'where are you at?' It tries to find out where a person is in the development of their relationship with God and their commitment to him. We took the idea from a similar booklet developed by Ichthus Fellowship in London, but adapted it for our own people and need.

The cell-group leader will give this booklet to the new member. After the member has had time to think about it and fill it out, the leader will chat with him or her to find out a little more about them. The matters they cover include: how the person became a Christian, how long ago that was, what discipling they have received, how they have been used by God in the past, how they may want to be used in the future, what their feelings are about evangelism, what their Bible-reading pattern is, and how they feel about their prayer life.

The cell-group leader needs to gauge how personal this should become. Some new members are just longing to talk about themselves and are willing to share everything at great depth. Others are hesitant and find it threatening to open up in this way. Sometimes this process takes a few weeks, but we have found it helpful to make sure that it is completed within the first month or two so that at least the cell-group leader knows something about the person, their experience and what their relationship with God is like.

The 'Journey Guide' also has a spiritual gifts questionnaire that enables the person to identify some of the gifts God has given them. Even if they have only just become a Christian we still ask them to complete this questionnaire as it will probably show up their natural talents. Then in a couple of years they will complete it again and see how God has developed those natural talents and given new gifts to them as well. They find it very exciting then to look back and see how God has changed them for the better over the years. Some are even surprised at this. One of our members was amazed to see he now had a gift of evangelism. He knew God had made it easy for him to chat about what Jesus had done for him, but he thought only people like Billy Graham had that particular gift.

Finally in the 'Journey Guide' there is an occult check list. Members are asked to tick off anything occult that they have been involved in from a long list. We have found this vital as it has never ceased to amaze me or the cell-group leaders what some people have been involved in. The list is very comprehensive and we continue to add to it as we hear of more and more occult activity in our area.

When any activity is identified we lead the person to repent of it and pray for there to be no residual bad effect in their lives.

When the new member has completed the 'Journey Guide' he or she may need specific prayer for something. Perhaps they suffer from some past hurt that needs healing. Perhaps they have sins they need to repent of. They may need specific repentance concerning some occult activity that they previously did not know was wrong. The cell-group leader will call someone else in to help in this prayer time. Often it is a member of the cell group, but occasionally it is the cell-group co-ordinator or perhaps myself.

Once the 'Journey Guide' has been completed, the new cell-group member is in a much better position to continue learning from the Lord. They are now more aware of the problems that have hindered them in the past. They have been led to repent of identified sins and have been prayed for to receive healing for certain hurts that have been unearthed and are seen still to be affecting the way they live.

Most people who complete this 'Journey Guide' are Christians. Just occasionally we have found people who we thought were Christians but who have actually shown by their answers to the 'Journey Guide' they they have not yet come to faith. The cell-group leader then has the privilege of leading that person to the Lord. This is a one-to-one meeting; there is no confrontation within the cell-group meeting as to whether the person is really a Christian or not. We have a policy of treating everyone as a Christian if they want to come to the cell group. If they want to point out that they are not, that is up to them, but it is not for us to put them on the spot in the meeting.

Building on the foundations

Our next tool in the training process is the 'Arrival Kit'. This is also based on the year of equipping at Faith Community Baptist Church. Since we produced it, a similar 'Arrival Kit' has been written by Ralph Neighbour. It is a foundations or basics course for each new member of the church to complete. They go through it with another, more experienced cell-group member who does not have to be the cell-group leader. One of the exciting developments for us has been to see Christians who have only known the Lord for a short time leading their friends who have recently come to the church through the 'Arrival Kit'.

In theory the 'Arrival Kit' is a twelve-week course but it sometimes takes a little longer due to time pressure in people's lives. The new cell-group member has five Bible readings for each week with notes to help. They meet with a cell-group member once a week to talk over what they have learned and to discuss any questions they may have. These twelve weeks cover six specific subjects.

The *first* subject is about relationships, and especially about how God wants to restore our relationship with him. It therefore deals with how we become Christians, what Jesus has done for us and how he wants us to function as members of his Church. The *second* part deals with the question of assurance of faith. The *third* looks at the authority of the Bible, especially in the light of reason, experience and tradition. The *fourth* area is Christian growth, and the battle that is to be encountered in this growth. We study the new nature and the old nature, and the need to put on the whole armour of God. Part *five* relates to the matter of our personal significance. Over the years we have seen this to be a key issue, as many of our members have a background of low self-esteem. People do not feel they are worth very much to God or the community. Even those who do not have this problem need to be aware of the place that achievement has in their lives. We have found Figures 10 and 11 helpful.

People who have little self-esteem are always striving to achieve so that others will accept them or that they can accept themselves (see Figure 10). The truth, however, is that we must know that we are accepted by God even before we have done anything (see Figure 11). 'God demonstrates his own love for us in this: while we were still sinners, Christ died for us' (Romans 5:8). That is the root of our personal significance. That then sustains us and enables us to achieve things for God and produce good spiritual fruit that will last. This is all displayed in the relationship of God the Father to Jesus, who said, 'You are my Son, whom I love; with you I am well pleased' before Jesus had even begun his ministry (Luke 3:22).

The *final* part of the 'Arrival Kit' deals with how God guides us and our need to look outwards. We have tried not to allow any new members to go more than a month or two into their Christian life without looking seriously at their witness. In practice, however, it is not usually necessary to encourage them to witness as new Christians are often very keen to tell others about what God has been doing in their lives. Nevertheless, it is very important that the Church presents witness as a normal part of Christian living. I believe that in the past we have not stressed this enough, so that regular and effective witness outside the body of the Church has become the exception rather than the rule. Not so now for the cell-group members at St John's.

Back to the Bible

These two stages of the process of equipping, the 'Journey Guide' and the 'Arrival Kit', are always done within the

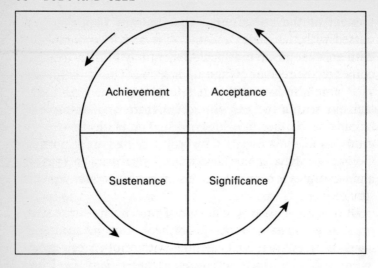

Figure 10. The cycle of low self-esteem

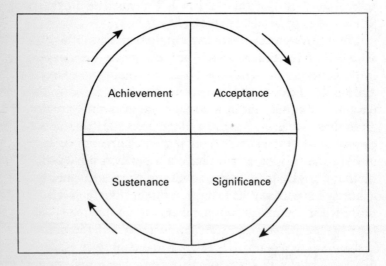

Figure 11. The cycle of high self-esteem

context of the cell groups. The 'Journey Guide' is discussed with the leader and the 'Arrival Kit' is completed with another group member. All the time this new member comes to the regular cell-group meeting. This is important as it emphasises personal relationships. It is one-to-one learning within the groups and therefore is an example of helping each other. It also shows how each member of the group from the newest to the oldest is important both to God and to the group. There are to be no also-rans or hangers-on. God wants to equip each person for his service.

Only recently, a new member of the church spoke with obvious enthusiasm about what she had been learning in her weekly 'Arrival Kit' meetings with another cell-group member. She told her cell-group members how God had sorted out her thinking about her relationship with him and the importance of God speaking to her through the Bible. Through the 'Arrival Kit' God was building sure foundations in her Christian life.

The next element of the equipping process is a little different. It is called 'Cover the Bible' and is adapted from material by Ralph Neighbour under that name.[10] Although I have been using someone else's material, this part of the equipping process has caused me the greatest amount of work. 'Cover the Bible' is a course that looks at the contents of the Bible book by book. There are detailed notes on each book of the Bible. It is partly history, partly theology, and partly about how God speaks through his word into the daily lives of Christians. There is also a script from Ralph Neighbour that is to be read onto tape by the pastor and used by members of the church in five-minute sections. There are five sections per week for fifty-two weeks. I spent many a long hour one winter recording this onto tape, but I do not regret one minute of it. Members can now have tapes that give them five minutes of Howard Astin speaking each day, five days a week, fifty-two weeks a year. My wife says this is more than she gets sometimes!

It was necessary to alter the script slightly so that it fitted our situation and culture. It was important that listeners heard the voice of their pastor rather than that of some stranger. It also enabled me to change certain parts of the script when there were examples I wanted to give, or certain emphases that I wanted to make. Sometimes there were parts of the theology that I wanted to change slightly, especially when it came to the interpretation of Revelation.

I wish I had been given this information about the Bible early in my Christian life. Certainly, people need some commitment to finish this course but those who have done so have found the reward is great. I believe those who have completed the course are no longer 'infants, tossed back and forth by the waves, and blown here and there by every wind of teaching and by the cunning and craftiness of men in their deceitful scheming' (Ephesians 4:14). There is a new interest in the Bible. For instance, a number of people have told me how they have regularly started reading the Old Testament. Before doing 'Cover the Bible' it had seemed confusing to them and they had not known how the different books related to each other. I even recall one memorable occasion when someone told me with great enthusiasm of his readings in Leviticus!

People are able to come to me and ask questions, and discuss in more detail matters that interest them. It can be a bit disconcerting on a Sunday when someone talks enthusiastically about what I've said to them that morning, only to find they are not talking about the sermon, but 'Cover the Bible'! I believe the benefit is great because every member of the church has ready access to a far greater depth of knowledge of the Bible than they could possibly have attained just by listening to sermons week by week. Also, they did not have to attend further meetings (praise the Lord) but could use the material as part of their daily quiet time with the Lord.

Special central courses

We try hard to keep all application of teaching within the cell-group structure but we have found that there are times when it is more effective to do some teaching centrally. We have held special weekends when groups have met together for training sessions. More recently, they have taken place on a Thursday and Friday night rather than over a weekend, because it has been difficult to get people to come on a Saturday. We try and run the first two, 'Spiritual Formation' (Basics) and 'Combined Harvesting' (Evangelism) each year. The other three ('Study the Bible for All It's Worth', 'Where on Earth Am I Going with God?' (about guidance), and 'Prayer, Fasting and Spiritual Warfare') we try and hold once every two years.

'Spiritual Formation' sessions are important in that we bring together all the new Christians who have joined over the last year. Most who attend will have completed the 'Journey Guide' and the 'Arrival Kit' and may well be involved in 'Cover the Bible'. Although they will have gathered some knowledge and expertise already, we find it necessary to look in some depth at certain areas of their relationship with the Lord that they are experiencing day by day. We look at the overall church strategy and the group structure and how their group plays its part. We look at the need to be filled with the Holy Spirit, the importance of their prayer life, and the fact that they are in a spiritual battle. We also give them some training on how to pray for others, especially for healing.

Although this is done centrally, the teaching at all times

relates back to their group setting and their experiences of group life. We have found that this course enables people to see how important their small-group life is, but it also encourages them by showing how they are part of a larger group of people who are involved in the same spiritual battle as themselves. In other words, there are many others in the church at the same stage in their relationship with God with whom they can empathise.

'Combined Harvesting' is about witnessing. We have found that people need help in building up their confidence to witness effectively to those around them. We chose the title to show that witness is a group activity which mobilises individuals. The course covers the biblical basis for witnessing, some aspects of whom we should be witnessing to, what makes a good testimony, and how to share the gospel effectively.

It has been encouraging over the years to see some who were fairly timid become effective witnesses as they begin to realise how God wants to use them. They see that they do have an ability to tell others about Jesus in a down-to-earth, ordinary but incisive way. The course has also helped to clear up the confusion between who is an evangelist and who is a witness. Some have been identified as evangelists on this course. Others have known that they were not evangelists but have realised for the first time that God wants to use them to 'gossip the gospel' to their neighbours, friends and relatives. They received a new confidence to do so. I recall one woman speaking to me of her surprise when she left the post office and realised she had just told the next person in the queue about how her life had changed for the better since she became a Christian.

In attending a cell group week by week, the members would have known something of the need to witness to people around them. By coming to this course they are able to pick up expertise and knowledge that they may never otherwise have received. The course complements the weekly programme of the cell group.

We developed the other three courses as we identified people's need for particular help. The first of these ('Study the Bible for All It's Worth') very much complements the 'Cover the Bible' course. It gives a bird's-eye view of the Bible and stresses the reliability of the Bible as God's word to us today. The course then becomes practical, asking why and how we should study the Bible. Then it looks at some traditionally difficult areas, such as questions of Church discipline, divorce, homosexuality and the role of women in the Church. In addition, we look at helpful ways to continue reading the Bible day by day, comparing published notes and even advocating 'Cover the Bible' if some have slipped through its net!

Guidance is often a problem with Christians, so we have developed a course on guidance called 'Where on Earth Am I Going with God?' In addition to looking at some of the principles of guidance, we also talk about worldwide mission, and have displays from many missionary organisations. We as a church are beginning to look at world mission much more seriously because we believe God is calling us to send people far and wide. We have a history of being rather near-sighted in our witness. This course therefore gives God the opportunity to plant the seed thought that a person might be called overseas to serve him.

The final course is more advanced, in that it looks again at prayer, but also teaches about fasting, intercession and further aspects of spiritual warfare. This has developed as our church has become more aware of the nature of the spiritual battle, not only in our area and city but also in our nation. We have seen a number of people called to be intercessors over the years, and are at present reappraising the role of the intercessor in relation to the cell-group structure. Usually intercessors are in different cell groups but they come together monthly to share what God has been saying to them and to pray together, perhaps about specific issues. As this course is run only periodically, some have used it as a refresher to look again at the fundamentals of prayer, fasting, spiritual warfare and the authority that we have in Christ in this spiritual battle.

There are battles raging around people in the spiritual realm that the cell-group leaders need to discern. Some battles are only won by prayer and fasting. Some are won only by persistent prayer and fasting. A group recently knew that the wife of one of the members should be prayed for specifically by the whole group, and this involved fasting. This wife was not a Christian and had been suffering from depression for some time. There was also evidence that she was seeing another man and the marriage was in great danger of ending. She had left home on occasions over the past six months. The group set aside time to pray and fasted one day a week for a couple of months. During that time the crisis in the marriage came to a head. The wife realised that she did not want to leave her husband and in effect pleaded to come home and try again. Prayer continues for this couple. The wife has still not become a Christian, although there are signs that she is now more willing to consider this than ever before. The battle continues.

Everyone is included

So far in this chapter I have tried to describe how a new member is equipped so that he or she is prepared for works of service. If you are to become a cell-group church, I believe it is necessary to take steps to equip all your existing members. It was very tempting for us to take these steps in the equipping process only with those who were joining us, but it was necessary to include all our existing members. Recently I read an article which described building a cell-group church as being like building a shed from second-hand wood. There was talk of yanking out rusty nails, hacking off rotting sections, smoothing out splinters, and shaping the wood for its new use. How the builder wished he had ordered all new timber! Here is the advantage of beginning a cell-group church from new. However, God had called us to lead the existing members into cell groups—rusty nails, splinters and all—and these courses helped us to sort out this wood for future use.

I can say that not all our existing members were used to being transparent about their lives or their relationship with God. Some now look back and see how they wore masks or played deception games. Some now see that they were hiding their real selves by way of evasion, or were prickly and unbending. By being involved in cell groups and by going through the equipping process, some of these tendencies were challenged and a number of people were given confidence to show their real selves. I think of one person in particular who was always so prickly that it was easy to upset them, even without doing a thing. It was as though no one could ever get near. However, a short time into cell-group life the fears that lay behind the prickliness started to come out into the open and were dealt with. God was able to touch that person with his love. 'Perfect love casts out all fear' (1 John 4:18). The cell group and the equipping process go hand in hand. The process is often the catalyst that provokes change within the context of the loving relationships in the cell group.

At the other extreme, we had those who could not stop 'sharing'. It was as if a cork had been let out of a bottle and everyone was then covered in verbal spray. Why did this person need to share so regularly and effusively? Again, the equipping process and cell group helped that person to see the effect they had on others; they turned them into timid spectators.

Like most other churches, we also had some people who regularly and forcefully raised particular theological issues. This was despite the fact that those issues had been raised for centuries with the Christian Church without ever being fully resolved! Through 'Cover the Bible' and 'Study the Bible for All It's Worth' these issues were looked at. I remember one person who was 'hung up' on a particular theological issue to such an extent that it stopped him witnessing. However, when there came the reminder at each cell-group meeting of the need to reach out, the cumulative effect over weeks and months was to sideline the theological issue so that the main work of the kingdom, namely making other disciples, could be achieved. He now does not see the issue as being important for him any more.

Others in our church struggled simply with being in relationship with others at a deeper level than before. For these people it has taken time to integrate fully into the group. But life in the cell group, meetings with the cell-group leader to look at their 'Journey Guide', and working through the 'Arrival Kit' with someone else have helped considerably. It has been a courageous step for some to have to come under the authority of a cell-group leader and to be in equal relationship with others within the group.

God called us to lead a whole church—with all the splinters, rusty nails and hard unbending wood—to become a new cell-group church. All were invited. Consequently we saw that the equipping process was not just to straighten out the new members of the church, but also to straighten out many of the existing members. It was a salutary process and very valuable.

CHAPTER 6

MAKING THE TRANSITION

If you have caught the cell-group church vision by now, other questions will be on your mind. What is your present church situation? How do you move from where you are at present to where you want to be? Will any transition be successful?

Here is a countdown of the transition process from ten to one, beginning with getting your thinking right even before there is any action. Some of these are based on our good experiences at St John's and some are based on our mistakes. All are based on what we believe God has said to us over our first four years of transition.

10. Watch your motives

Why go down the route of becoming a cell-group church? Is it because there is so much talk about cell churches that you are simply jumping on a bandwagon, or do you have a real desire to see a growing, effective church?

Neither of these reasons is really valid. There is only one important reason to pursue the cell model and that is obedience. I needed to know that God had spoken to us at St John's and told us to become a cell-group church. It is a vision from God for evangelism through every member and for ministry through every member. I was so utterly convinced that God had given this vision to the church that when we failed in certain ways we were able to get up and try again. My warning is that if your motive is anything other than obedience to such a calling, don't do it.

Obviously, we all face obstacles and set-backs. At these times I have had to look at myself closely. When I felt I was dragging some of the leaders into a new way of doing things that would cost them dearly, I had to know that God had said this was the way we should go. There is no doubt that the cell-group church demands personal sacrifice and reorientation. Probably the biggest church in the world—Yoido Full Gospel Church in Seoul, Korea, which now has over 750,000 members—is based on cell principles. Yet David Yonggi-Cho, the pastor, had many problems in implementing the cell structure in the years after 1964 when God had told him to do it. It took him ten years to get the majority of the members involved in the cell groups. Along the way he needed to know that God had called him to do it, and he needed to be obedient.

There is danger, too, if my main motive is to grow a big church and thereby become an influential leader in the kingdom. This question of motive is not just for the senior leader of a church, but for every group leader, and really for every member. This is so important that in the summer of 1997 I gave each member of the leadership team at St John's the opportunity to reappraise their situation and to hear from God afresh that he had called them into leadership. It was not good enough to know that their vicar wanted them to be leaders or even that they themselves wanted to be leaders. They had a chance to step down. I took a big risk—I could have ended up leading eighteen groups! Fortunately, God had different ideas and most of the leaders have continued in the task. It is a matter of examining our heart and checking our motives.

9. Pay the price—willingly

The cell-church model involves more than structural change. It requires every member of the church to change, and that starts with the leader 'downwards'. God knows that I am willing to change in theory but I have to change in practice. I have to ask myself, 'Am I really willing to reach out personally to those who are lost? Am I willing to love the people around me and to share Christ with them? Am I willing to make an effort to get to know people who are not yet Christians?' Like many leaders, I seem to have spent most of my time with Christians over the last few years. I now need to change my life-style so that I have time outside church activities to make new friends and relate to people who live nearby.

This has by no means been easy, because I also need to spend time in prayer. Prayer and life-style evangelism go together, and as a leader I have needed to show by example that I value these. The question is whether I have succeeded. But if you don't want to be transformed yourself, forget transforming your church. John Wesley once asked, 'Why are we not more holy? Chiefly because we are enthusiasts, looking for the ends without the means. We want lively churches, thriving evangelistic programmes, glorious worship and social sensitivity, but we are often not prepared for the personal renewal which must undergird these things.' Each of us needs to get serious with God in this transition time. That involves repentance, a real turning away from things known to be wrong, in order to live out Jesus' life-style. It involves prayer and it involves 'being Jesus' to those around us who are at present lost in sin. This may mean practical help or encouragement, or even challenge and conviction. But for us it often means sacrifice.

8. Change the values before the vision

I think I did a good job four-and-a-half years ago in selling the vision to the church. Yet I see now that what is really needed is a change of values before there can be a change of vision.

The values of the cell-group church are found first in prayer, the developing of our love relationship with and for God. Secondly, they are found in the 'body life' of the church, whereby we learn to love each other within the fellowship. Thirdly, they are found in evangelism, as we receive from God his compassion for the lost.

In the six months leading up to the launch of our cell groups in autumn 1993, I preached on these topics—but without fully realising their fundamental importance. I only did it as I preached about the vision, which revolved around the proposed change of structure. Yet people cannot grasp the vision without really being aware of the need for change in their values. There is a difference between agreeing to a change because it is a way of helping the church to grow, and agreeing to that change because we believe God wants to change us and thereby motivate us to love him more and to love people around us who are lost without him.

It was therefore important for us to do further work on this when the groups began. We used the *I Factor*[11] within the new cell groups to re-emphasise the foundational points of caring for each other and reaching out to those who are not yet Christians. The short course helped people to identify who God wanted them to witness to, to see what he was already doing in the lives of these people, and to think through practical ways in which to show God's love to them. The course also helped members to explain Christianity to others effectively and to give details of how they themselves became Christians. It gave a new awareness to group members of how they as a group could reach out to those around. The foundations of a cell-group church are in its values and not its structure. You need to lay these foundations well.

7. Pray and then pray

The change to a cell-group structure seems to be the most important thing, yet that is not the whole truth. It is an important change, but it is not all-important. Prayer is vital. The cell-group structure is like an electrical appliance. It can have a far-reaching effect (just as a television shows a picture, or an electric fire gives heat) but it needs to be plugged in first. Our cell-group structure first of all has to be plugged in to God's power before looking outwards at the needs of the world. You will see an amazing difference 'before' and 'after'.

So my plea is that you should not get serious about creating cells unless you are also willing to get serious about seeking God in prayer.

Many pastors and leaders know that their prayer life is rather inadequate but may well try and justify this lack of prayer to themselves by saying that they are too busy to pray. When talking to lay church members, I have been amazed at how they take it for granted that their pastors pray regularly and at length. By knowing my own past prayer life and talking to other pastors, I know that this is not the case, and yet some still put up a good argument as to why they cannot pray regularly or at length.

It is only recently, since we formed cell groups, that God has given me the discipline to get up earlier than I would like in order to spend vital time with him before the busyness of the day begins. He used the book *Too Busy Not to Pray* by Bill Hybels to change the way I thought about my prayer life.[12] For example, I started to write down some of my prayers. This helped my concentration enormously and it is now good to be able to look back and see which prayers have been answered and in what ways.

To say we are too busy to pray runs against the model of God-centred living shown by Jesus. He was busy, but he spent time with his Father. There were many people around him seeking his attention but he left them to go and pray by himself (Luke 5:16).

This emphasis on prayer is also evident in the book of Acts when the early Christians came together. Is it a coincidence that the Holy Spirit then came in power in many different ways? Many people were saved, Christians experienced the Holy Spirit giving them boldness and faith, buildings were shaken, angels were seen, instructions were given, prisoners were released, visions were given and all manner of signs and wonders were evident.

There may be other factors in Britain in the 1990s, but we see very few signs and wonders or phenomenal Church growth. It is a brave person who says that the situation here has little to do with our paucity of prayer. I fervently believe that the cell-group structure is a powerful tool that God wants to use, but it must be based on his power. Are you willing to change your prayer life?

6.   How do you start—in your church?

Some would urge you to take the whole church through the transition together. Others would urge you to start small, with one cell. In fact, there can be variations even within these two positions. The key must be to know what God is saying to you in your church, in your situation.

At St John's we believed God was calling us to change the whole church and we knew it would take time. Look-ing back, we can also see many disadvantages in doing this. One of the obvious ones is that we were learning as we went along and did not have the experience of a prototype or of another group to learn from. Car manufacturers build a prototype of a new model before they mass-produce it. This enables them to work out what the problems are. If there is not a prototype, then they can expect a lot of factory recalls.

Consequently, it must be said that churches that rush into a cell model by skipping through the research and investigation stages may well suffer from a number of recalls as they discover gaps and other missing components. We certainly found gaps in our training programme as we did not have enough apprentice leaders in place as the groups began.

On the other hand, we did not have the problem of seeing one part of the church 'go for it' while another part did not. I know from speaking to other ministers that it is very difficult to keep two church structures going side by side. One of the keys to the success of the cell-group structure is for there to be no competition from programmes operating across the church such as men's meetings, women's meetings, an evangelism team, and so on. David Yonggi-Cho, pastor of Yoido, says the same:

> You must change the basic structure of your church. Many churches are failing in their cell ministry because they have not changed the basic church structure, for instance: Sunday school, women's groups, etc. You can't graft the cell system into the old traditional church ministry. The structure must be changed. This change is very difficult. If you don't change the basic structure, then the cell system will only be an added ministry to your church which will soon fizzle away.[13]

Unfortunately, the church is not exempt from the fact that bad news travels faster than good. Although there is the wonderful testimony of those involved in cell groups that they now have a renewed purpose, a new excitement in the gospel and a new passion in their Christian lives, some can also hear that being involved in a cell group is hard work, costly and frustrating, and therefore resist it.

I do not wish to advocate either the whole-church transition method or the start-small prototype method, or any in between. You must hear from God as to how he wants you to start in your particular circumstances.

5.   'Do not look down on [the children]' (Matthew 18:10)

When Jesus spoke these words he was making more than a point about status in the kingdom. He had taken a little child and placed him in the midst of the disciples, and was speaking about the very nature of the Church as the family of God.

Children are not potential members of the Church, or indeed the Church of tomorrow. They belong now and have the rights of the kingdom now. They are therefore not to be on the edge of what the local church is doing and not to be hived off to a high-class baby-sitting service while the adults get on with real church.

Our transition to a cell-group church has made a big difference to the way in which I and other members of St John's have looked at the ministry to children and the ministry by children. They are to be fully within the family of the Church, with loads of spiritual aunts and uncles, brothers and sisters.

The adults also provide models for the children: this is how to be a father, or a mother, or a teenager, or someone who is a single adult or indeed a senior citizen. They can have a relationship with those adults, learning from them in conversations and in the answers to their many questions. They are also needed by the adults to remind them that they are still children of God themselves. Do they have the faith of the child, and the questioning that is based on eagerness rather than scepticism?

In the plan to take a church towards becoming a cell-group church it is necessary to know what God is saying about the children and youth. I have found it depressing to talk with people who are interested in the cell-group model yet who never ask questions about the children. They assume that the model is really only for adults. That is far from the truth.

Children need to be involved in a small group. There they can develop their faith and grow spiritually. There they can find friendship, encouragement and support. It is a place for their questions and for sharing their troubles. Within the group they learn to serve, to pray and to hear from God personally. They start displaying the spiritual gifts that have been given to them by their God.

The question you must face is which variation within the cell-church structure God would have you adopt. Although there are maybe more, there are certainly two that need to be considered.

Cells for children

The first is the one that we have adopted from the beginning. All our children and youth have been in cell groups since autumn 1993. We have cell groups for the under-fives, for the five to nine-year-olds, for those over nine, and for teenagers.

Here they meet with their peers to discuss problems in their own forum. Even those aged eighteen months start getting involved in the worship and activities of the cell group. By the time they are about five years old they begin to pray for each other and to be concerned for each other. As they grow older, they start praying earnestly and effectively for their situations. These can be school tests, or families, or bad habits, or journeys they are going on, or their pets, or the need to bring others to know Jesus.

It is no longer Sunday school, and there is no talk of teachers or lessons, classes or pupils, but instead of leaders, groups and members. It becomes a bit like a family, where they pick up a knowledge of life and how the Bible is relevant to their lives.

It is wonderful to hear our children's leaders speak about how these youngsters could now have at least ten years' vital relationship with Jesus before they reach the questioning years of their teens. I am sure that the temptation to drift away from church life will be so much weaker as they will have the experience of a relationship with Jesus that has been tested over time.

We have found that the ideal number for a children's group is about eight; it should not get larger than twelve. Then it must multiply, and so it is necessary for an apprentice leader to be there ready. These groups do grow, even when they operate as ours do on a Sunday morning when it's perhaps more difficult to attract the previously unchurched. New members have joined, and the existing members have to learn to make them welcome by, for instance, not embarrassing those who don't have as good a knowledge of the Bible as their own. They have had to understand when some can only attend spasmodically due to their family circumstances. They have had to see it as their responsibility to do the welcoming.

All-age cells

The other model is of integrated or inter-generational cells. I do not have much experience of these, but I do know that many cell-group churches around the world adopt this method. Here the adults and the children of those adults meet together and worship as a cell. Quite often they then pray for each other and during the edification/application part of the meeting, the children will have their own activity and application, or will just go off and do their homework or even go to sleep! The idea is that all awake members of the meeting come back together at the end, to look outwards from the group as a whole.

Sometimes these cell groups meet at an earlier time than would be usual for an evening meeting. Quite often a meal is part of the meeting and there is therefore the informal mixing of all members of the group. Sometimes one particular adult is called to run activities for the children as part of the evening. Sometimes the whole group will have a 'children's evening' or on occasion there will be a child-free night when all parents get a baby-sitter.

There are many advantages of these all-age groups. The first is that it is so much easier for the children to get to know the adults who are in their parents' cell. They become their friends as well as their parents' friends. They also act as role-models for the children. The adults, likewise, are enriched and challenged by the contribution of the children. It can be easier for new adults to join the group because their children can come too.

There can, however, be problems. With children present as well as adults, a large room is needed to accommodate the numbers, with possible access to another room for some of the children's activities. There also needs to be supervision of the children. The children often want to have their own cell group with their peers. Sometimes an adult group will not have enough children in it to enable this to happen. Sometimes the age range is so great that they cannot really share together. Something is then lost in the whole development of maturity and gifting within the child over the years. In addition, the adults may not wish to share any difficult moral or ethical problem that they are facing with children present.

We have now taken the step to link particular adult cells with selected children's or youth cells, so they can sometimes meet together and support each other in prayer.

What is important is that the children and youth are seen as a vital part of the church, not merely an added extra to the main church structure. Before you proceed, make sure 'you do not look down on these little ones'.

4. Train the leaders

Jim Egli, a director of Touch Outreach Ministries, has said, 'The cell model is not a small group strategy; it is a leadership strategy.' He is right. The delegation of leadership is part and parcel of the cell-church model. You must be prepared to invest in the leadership of the church. A careful examination of Jesus' ministry in Mark's Gospel shows that he spent perhaps half his time in leadership training by interacting, teaching and mentoring the inner circle of the twelve disciples. In fact, the cell gives training even before members take up leadership positions. Members will be involved in caring, organising, supporting and praying. This enables the cell-group leader and the co-ordinators to spot potential leaders over a period of time. A combination of role-modelling and instruction must be in place in order to prepare leaders for the expansion of the cell-group church.

In hindsight we recognise that there can be no short cuts in the training or the support system for leaders. We can also see that if we succeed in preparing leaders, then the cell group will succeed. The strength of the church will depend on the number and the strength of the leaders, which in turn relies on our ability to identify and train new leaders.

Beware the temptation to try out potential leaders by

letting them lead children's or youth cells prior to adult cells. Over the four years of transition, we have come to see that in comparison to a children's or youth cell, leading an adult cell is easy! We have seen that the need for commitment and the ability to communicate vision are far greater when leading the younger ones. We have also tried strongly to counter any suggestion that a leader is of a higher status when leading an adult rather than a children's or youth cell. In God's eyes this is the opposite of the truth.

3. Want to learn

People who are still eager to learn prove to be the most successful cell-group church leaders. They are constantly looking for new ideas and new insights on how to improve the way they do things. With this desire goes a humility and an acknowledgement that they have a lot to learn. They don't mind learning from people in other churches, other denominations, other countries, or indeed from those who are younger than themselves.

It has been tempting at times to get defensive about what we have done and what we have achieved at St John's when faced with new ideas of how to proceed or even suggestions that we may have done things wrong. I must stay open to learning more and more from God about this whole subject. Quite often God speaks through others. 'Pride only breeds quarrels, but wisdom is found in those who take advice' (Proverbs 13:10).

You must then go to great lengths to learn, both before beginning any transition process and also during the time of change. That may mean travelling to other churches, reading books, or attending conferences. It may just mean being willing to acknowledge mistakes and wrong turnings, and then changing.

2.   Have a one-track mind

Larry Stockstill, the pastor of a church I once visited in Baton Rouge, Louisiana, said, 'It is hard to be on a diet and eat your regular meals, too.' You cannot really build cells along with everything else a church normally does. Even if you begin a cell-group church by the prototype method mentioned in point 6 above, before too long other programmes and activities the church is involved in will either have to change in order to come within the life of the cells or come to an end.

But why are cell-group church ministers so adamant about the elimination of any competition to the cell life? The reason is that if you have any extensive programmes beside the cells, the programmes will contend with the cell system for time, energy, leadership and prayer. If you deplete your leadership pool with other programmes, your cells will get too big and you will not be able to multiply. They will stagnate. So it is a fundamental issue for anyone thinking of starting a cell-group church, but it is also a vital issue for the cell-group church when it is up and running.

One of the most unpopular steps we took soon after the adoption of the cell-group structure was to discontinue our evening service. This was particularly unpopular as many people attended it. It also enjoyed a freedom of worship not experienced in the mornings and a greater opportunity for praying for each other without constraints of time. However, we believed God was specifically saying that those attributes should in fact be in our morning services and that people needed an extra night either to meet informally in cell groups, to spend time with individuals in their $\phi ikos$, or just to relax and spend time with the family. Our cell groups meet weekly and in practice there are other commitments linked with the cell each week. Some members are doing the 'Arrival Kit' with new members. The whole group may set aside some other time for prayer. Then there is the need to spend time with non-Christian friends and relatives. Therefore having a regular evening service would become counter-productive to the whole vision for the church, taking up vital time for the cell-group members.

Another factor was that we believed God was leading us to develop the worship within the cell-group meeting so that people's worship and prayer needs were met in the groups. So we needed to eliminate competition.

The challenge is for you to examine minutely the programmes of the church and, whenever necessary, eliminate them carefully and prayerfully. If this is not done, your cells will fail.

1. Love people more than the vision

One of the biggest mistakes leaders make in the transition to cells is to love the vision more than the people. Sometimes the vision becomes so important to them that people are seen to be a means to an end, rather like the zealous evangelists who allegedly have notches on the spine of their Bible for all those that they have led to Christ. We can see the growth of leaders as vital to make the vision work. We can treat cell-group members like pawns in the strategy, requiring them to love each other within the group and love those outside the group. Even those who are not yet Christians can become numbers in the Church growth game.

Such attitudes do not display Jesus' compassion either for the lost or for the members of his Church or his inner circle of disciples.

The Pharisees exalted God's Law to a lofty position. They thought people existed merely to serve the Law. Jesus had the reverse mind-set. 'The Sabbath was made for man, not man for the Sabbath' (Mark 2:27). The same can be said of vision. The vision is made for people, not people for the vision.

If the vision of leading your church into a cell-group church is primarily seen as a Church growth strategy, then you will experience frustration and disappointment. Instead, it is a vision for the people, that God's people may be liberated in their walk with him, and those who are lost may find entry into Jesus' Church.

Finally, I need to point out that the period of transition is not an easy time. It is interesting to note that the word 'transition' is used for a particular point during childbirth when a mother-to-be is likely to react very negatively to what is happening. She says things like: 'I can't go on', 'I don't want this baby', 'I hate my husband', and the like. Obviously, the phrases used by those involved in birthing a cell-group church may well be different, but they may be equally negative at times. Following this parallel, it is useful to remember that these negative thoughts are soon forgotten by the mother when the baby is actually born.

Do dream big dreams. Let God also expand your capacity to care. Follow this countdown, ten to one, but realise that behind each and every point is the command of God to love him with all your heart, mind, soul and strength and to love your neighbour (and members) as yourself. To change into a cell-group church is stretching, frustrating and disappointing, but also exciting and fulfilling. If God tells you to do it, then do it. Has God spoken? If he has, then obey.

CHAPTER 7

THE WORLDWIDE PICTURE

'Cells can't work in Britain.' That was often said to me or implied by other British church leaders when they heard that we were moving towards being a cell-group church at St John's. They often conceded that cell-group churches were working effectively in other parts of the world, such as the Far East, South America or Africa. Many were doubtful, however, that cell-group church life could ever fit into our culture here.

Surprisingly perhaps, in the light of all I have written so far, I believe the jury is still out. I am unsure if the cell-group church *will* work effectively in this country, but I have no doubt that it *can* work. To say it does not fit into our culture is, I believe, untenable for biblical, historical and social reasons. The Bible records that a small group movement turned every culture it touched 'upside down'. Christian small group movements have periodically renewed the vitality of the Western Church. The Methodist class system begun by John Wesley was one. Today many kinds of small groups are popular in this country, including groups for therapy, fitness, adult education, New Age, and even street gangs. In fact, some people are not only happy to become part of a group, but they will even pay money to do so! It is not the resistance of non-Christians to small groups, but the resistance of the institutional church to change that hinders the growth of the movement.

It will be profitable to make a short survey of what God is doing across the world in the cell-group church movement. This is very far from an exhaustive study, but is based on information I have gleaned from reading and by visits to cell-group churches in Singapore and the United States. There is evidence that the Holy Spirit is at work across many nations and cultures in a very similar way.

The Far East phenomenon

Whenever the cell-group church movement is discussed, reference is invariably made to Dr David Yonggi-Cho and his church, the Yoido Full Gospel Central Church in Seoul, Korea. He began meeting in 1958 with five people in a tent. When the church started to grow large, he began the cell-group structure in 1964. By 1989 there were 600,000 people in the church, growing to 750,000 in the early 1990s and now approaching a million.

We cannot say that this phenomenal growth in church membership is purely down to the cell-group structure. Although David Yonggi-Cho argues fervently that it is a fundamental factor, he claims that it was the emphasis on prayer that changed the spiritual climate in Korea. When speaking in Nottingham, England, in March 1995 he talked of how the 'skies were clear' over Korea, meaning that God and his angels had won the battles in the spiritual realm over Korea so that God was able to bring many people to faith in that land. Consequently, he is in effect arguing for a combination of an emphasis on prayer and a cell-group church structure so as to facilitate growth.

There are now dozens of large churches in Korea, but all the largest are cell-group churches. The world's largest

Presbyterian church is in Seoul, and is a cell-group church. Likewise, the largest Methodist church in the world is a cell-group church in Korea.

David Yonggi-Cho is a fervent advocate of the cell-group model. He says 'By following the guidelines I have presented . . . you can bring the miracles of home cell groups and church growth to your congregation.'[14] He also states that large churches must break down into small cell groups if they are to continue to grow. My mind boggles at the idea of a church of one million when in Britain a church of over 200 people seems quite large, but I long for the day when it happens!

In other parts of South-East Asia there are also examples of thriving cell-group churches. The Shepherd Community in Hong Kong; the Hope of Bangkok Church in Thailand, led by Dr Kriengsak; and the Faith Community Baptist Church in Singapore which hosts the International Cell Church Conference each year, are probably the best known.

The Faith Community Baptist Church in Singapore is led by Lawrence Khong, who has worked closely with Ralph Neighbour since the late 1980s to implement cell-group church principles. Ralph Neighbour's theories on cell-church structure had been written for many years before they were put into practice fully in a church in Singapore in the 1980s. That church grew to 4,500 people in 1990 and now has a membership of over 7,000.

When I visited this church in 1993, I was immediately struck by how efficient and effective it was in all aspects of church life. As I talked to some of the members, it became clear that they understood the structure of the church. They knew who their cell-group leader and their senior pastor were, and also who their cell-group leader was responsible to and what the whole vision of the church was.

The visit to the church office was awe-inspiring. There

was a room for each zone of cell groups, with bar charts for each cell group within the zone. Most zones were geographical areas although there were also zones for the students, people doing military service, and those involved in the preparation of music and drama for the worship services. On a Saturday morning, the senior pastor, Lawrence Khong, could walk into any room and see from the bar chart how many people were at each cell group that week. The cell-group leaders had not only reported on their meetings, but that information had been processed to give an up-to-date picture of the health of the church measured by attendance at the cell groups.

Maybe this regimented cell structure particularly appeals to the Singaporeans. Their society as a whole is very structured. Even your parking tickets and speeding fines are automatically deducted from your next monthly pay cheque! The young men still do military service for two years and, due to the lack of space on the island, living accommodation is usually in high-rise blocks. The cell group model fits well into this society, even down to the ready-made community within each tower block where one or two cell groups meet. One of the visions for FCBC is for there to be at least one cell group within each tower block of Singapore by the year 2000.

However, I was also challenged by how business-like these Christians were in living out their faith. They reminded me of the early Church in their dedication to 'duty' in winning their neighbours for Christ. Was this attitude only due to the Singaporean culture, or was God wanting to speak to the West through his church in this former British colony? They did not see evangelism as an optional extra. The cell-group members were serious in working out a strategy for bringing their friends and relatives to know Jesus. They were faithful in passing on reports of their meetings and prayer times to the leadership of the church. Here, I felt, was a model for the church in the West. In comparison, we could be seen as primarily a church of attenders rather than a functioning army empowered by God's Holy Spirit to win battles for him.

The Latin American dimension

On the other side of the world, it surprised me to find phenomenal cell-church growth in Colombia and Peru. I don't often hear much of the church in these countries. Some of us may have heard of the revivals taking place in Argentina, but the International Charismatic Mission in Bogota, Colombia, with its vision to have 30,000 cell groups by 31 December 1997 was news to me.

Then there is the San Salvador La Mission Christiana Elim in El Salvador. It has at least 116,000 people attending 5,300 cells. On the days of united celebration, 600 of the city's buses are rented by the cell groups to get their members along. Both these churches visited Yoido Full Gospel Central Church in Korea in the mid 1980s but specifically contextualised what they learnt to their own cultural situation. For instance, the cell-group structure was formed with a mind to their geographical areas and their poorer church membership. They came to pray not on a 'prayer mountain' as in Korea, but in smaller group locations over a wider area.

In the Love Alive Church in Tegucigalpo, Honduras, the leaders of the church say that ninety-five per cent of their 7,500 members meet in their 850 cells. Other notable cell churches are the Christian Centre in Guayaguil, Ecuador, where 5,000 meet in 1,600 cells, and the Living Altar Church in Lima, Peru, where 6,500 members come together in 550 cells each week.

Joel Comiskey, who worked for five years in Ecuador with the Christian and Missionary Alliance, studied these

Latin American churches. He notes several trends. First of all, the cell-group ministry is the backbone of the church. The cell groups are the church itself and not added extras. Although the churches are very large in number, the individual cell groups are all linked to specific celebrations where they hear the senior pastor's weekly message. Cell members of each of these large churches have an awareness of sharing the same vision for the whole church. They place great emphasis on leadership training. In his survey, Comiskey questioned 400 leaders and found that sixty-eight per cent had experienced multiplication of their cell group at least once, and forty per cent more than once. Continued leadership training was a priority. He found that in the International Charismatic Mission Church in Bogota, 3,000 potential leaders were on a three-month course when he visited.

The overall impression given by these Latin American churches is that they see themselves as part of a strategic evangelistic force. Yet I have never heard it suggested that this dedication to duty is a fundamental part of their culture. It is also not just these churches that are growing. There is a move of God across South America. We see vast numbers of people becoming Christians. A mind-blowing report came to me of a church in Buenos Aires in Argentina where new members are told which of the eleven church services they should attend on a Sunday. Services happen every two hours with a two-hour break in the middle of the night to clean the church. We also hear of churches across the denominations working together evangelistically in most of the major cities across the continent. Invariably, cell groups are part of the structure of the churches involved in promoting and harnessing this growth.

Finally, there are the Base Ecclesial Communities which, in the main, emanate from the Catholic wing of the Church. These reportedly began in Brazil in 1956, and those that have traced the beginnings of the movement quote the words of an old lady: 'Christmas Eve,' she complained, 'all three Protestant churches were lit up and full of people . . . and the Catholic church closed and dark! . . . because we couldn't get a priest.' The question naturally arose as to why everything should come to a standstill simply because there was no priest. It led to an initiative in Rio de Janeiro that has spread widely throughout South America and beyond. In some cases they still are a testimony to the sovereign move of God in bypassing restrictive church structures. However, now these small community groups are adopted and promoted by those in the leadership of the church. Indeed, the growth was greatly encouraged by the meetings of the Latin American bishops in Colombia in 1968, Mexico in 1979 and Santo Domingo in 1992. Some say there are now approximately 200,000 such groups in South America. They bring Christians together in community to reach out to their neighbours and friends and to make a Christian impact on the community. They are often concerned with justice and peace, and the plight of the poor and the marginalisation of the under-privileged.

Cells in Africa

The picture is also similar in Africa. There is a spiritual awakening occurring across the continent. People are spiritually hungry and there is a battle in many of the African states between Islam and Christianity to meet this need. There are many thriving cell-group churches, one of the best known being that pastored by Dion Robert in Abidjan in the Ivory Coast. He still has his headquarters in Abidjan, but now has a network of churches in every major city and dozens of villages within the nation. The church itself was launched in 1975 but became a fully developed cell-group church in 1983. The membership then went from 638 in 1983 to 23,000 in 1991, and the membership is now nearer 100,000.

Cell groups in this church now multiply approximately every three months, which means that leadership training is one of the highest priorities. The greatest challenge that comes from this church is the amazing commitment shown by the members. Some travel for a whole day to reach their respective weekly celebrations. What a contrast to us in Britain, where travelling half an hour in a comfortable car to attend church is about the limit. Again, there is a businesslike attitude to evangelism and a depth of community spirit within their cell groups.

Cells in Western cultures

Cell-church growth is not restricted to the non-Western cultures. There are now cell-group churches in Australia, New Zealand, South Africa and the United States. Ian Freestone, a Church Army officer with Ruach Neighbourhood Churches in Sydney, Australia, has been planting churches on cell-group principles for some years. He has also published a short description of his experiences in *A New Way of Being Church*.[15]

In South Africa it would appear that the cell-group church movement is about to take off in a very big way. In 1993, 100 pastors from most of South Africa's denominations spent a month at the Faith Community Baptist Church in Singapore, and have been training other pastors since that time. Over 200 churches and 900 delegates have attended from every denomination and racial grouping. The oldest and biggest Pentecostal church in South Africa, the Apostolic Faith Mission, with its 1,050 local churches, has embraced the cell-church movement and a good percentage of these local churches are already beginning to make the transition.

This enthusiasm for the cell-church movement in South Africa has spilled over into Zambia where 1,000 pastors came together in August 1996 to look more deeply at changing church structures and planting churches on a cell-group model. These 1,000 pastors were literate, and were then trained so that they could pass on what they had been taught to 10,000 more pastors who were largely illiterate. Dion Robert from the Ivory Coast came to help in this training.

The initial reaction to cell-group churches in the United States has been the same as I found in the UK: 'Cell groups won't work here.' Evidence is now emerging to show that this is not true. However, there do seem to be some particular cultural barriers in many churches across the United States that hinder the ready acceptance of the cell-church principles.

Rick Warren, the senior pastor of Saddleback Valley Community Church in Orange County, California, has said, 'For a church to grow, both the pastor and the people must give up control. The people must give up control of the leadership, and the pastor must give up control of the ministry. Otherwise, either party can become a bottleneck for growth.' The traditional American pastor can control his church members and the members can control the pastor. Pastors of cell-group churches are no exception to the control mechanism and neither are cell-group leaders.

Some pastors feel it is very dangerous to delegate leadership within the church, and it is a characteristic of many American churches that the pastor should be under the firm control of the 'church board'. David Yonggi-Cho once spoke about such a situation. 'Anything that destroys personal independence and the individual's personality and responsibility is from the devil. God never created us to be puppets. He gave us personalities to be developed into loving sons and daughters living in relationship with him. Our home cell groups are designed to promote that relationship.' Cell groups therefore can be used either to control God's people or to release God's people.

Another factor is that some American Christians (like some British Christians) have swallowed the 'holy man' and 'holy building' myths. In other words, every Sunday morning they expect to find a holy man in a holy building who will administer to their needs. Some expect the holy man to be a counsellor who must be available twenty-four hours a day. Consequently, rather than becoming disciples and ministers, these well-meaning Christians are merely consumers of ministry.

Other commentators have suggested that quite often American churches have forgotten the mandate to reach the lost. C. T. Studd, the famous missionary, said, 'I do not wish to live 'neath sound of church or chapel bell, I want to run a rescue shop within a yard of hell.' Instead of being witnesses (Acts 1:8), some who regularly attend church are just partakers of complacent 'come to bless me' meetings. The cell-group movement has at its heart this evangelistic thrust that challenges more comfortable Christians to their roots.

These commentators go further and say that many of the Christians attending church in the United States lack desperation for God. They believe in him and come to worship him, but in their hearts they also think they can live their lives fairly well without daily reference to him. In some of the churches on other continents, there is a genuine hunger for God within believers. They believe that if God doesn't show up it is all over! New wineskins (new cells) must be regularly filled with new wine (a fresh experience of Jesus).

Having said all this concerning America, there are signs that God is now at work bringing many of his people back to the fundamentals. A pastor in Modesto, California commented that many with a history of 'church-going' almost needed a second conversion to become alive in the Spirit and to apply afresh the fundamentals of living as Christians. He emphasised the need to have loving relationships with God, with others, and particularly with the lost. His church, the First Baptist Church in Modesto, is making the transition into cell groups, and this process is proving to be a key factor for many existing members who are now coming spiritually alive. The cell-group model is working well in this predominantly white, middle-class church.

One of the largest cell-group churches in America is the Bethany World Prayer Center in Baker, Baton Rouge, Louisiana. The pastor, Larry Stockstill, has seen his church grow at a phenomenal rate since it adopted the cell-group structure. There are now about 10,000 members representing all strands of society. There are rich and poor, educated and uneducated, professional and non-professional, black and white all working together. This area of Louisiana has a church-going tradition but most churches have a membership of between thirty and fifty. They are also homogeneous, being either white or black, and often based around a particular family. This church at Baker therefore stands out like a beacon with its cross-cultural cell-group communities. In addition, the church reaches beyond its city boundaries and has missionaries serving in all continents of the world.

Another church that stands out as an example of the cell-group church in America is the New Life Fellowship in Queens, New York. Here the pastor, Peter Scazzero, has about 750 members who come from forty-six different racial groupings. The cell groups sometimes follow racial distinctions, but they are often mixed with people from different racial backgrounds and cultures. Peter Scazzero believes that this reflects God's desire for his church to cut across traditional social boundaries. This church shows that the cell-group strategy can work with members of different races and cultures. Perhaps more importantly, it demonstrates God's concern for people to be in community with others of a different race or culture.

Another leader of this church suggests that the movement towards cells reflected a move in American society against the 'rugged individualism' that has been particularly prevalent this century. Now there is much more desire to be part of a community. The emphasis is on relationship rather than the role of doing 'jobs' in church. Often the church in America has been based on who does what. 'You do this, you do that, I'll do this . . . let's make this thing work!' This appealed to middle-class people as it was more task oriented. The move to relationship was a challenge to many, but more and more are becoming open to it.

The British cell scene

Finally, what of the situation in Britain? Recently, I was involved in a Consultation within the Anglican Church to look at some of the new trends within churches. I discovered that church members were being led into cell groups from two completely different perspectives but coming to a similar vision. One can be said to be a bottom-up movement, the other top-down.

There is a grass roots movement occurring in which Christians come together in cells irrespective of traditional church structure. It has much more in common with the Base Ecclesial Communities that have so flourished in Brazil, Argentina and other South American countries. In some cases they are a reaction to the traditional structures that have not encouraged close relationships within the church and have neglected the call to mission. They follow a desire to be in community with other Christians. Often these communities have had a defined calling to specific social action within the community. Such a community has grown up in an area of inner-city Plymouth. The local Anglican church was not able to give a minister to the area, but rather than accepting that there would be no church presence on their housing estate, local Christians began meeting together regularly, both to worship and to meet some of the social needs of the area.

The other perspective comes from church leaders who are beginning to detect God's call to change traditional church structures so that members begin meeting in cell groups. These cells then in turn become small communities and take on many of the aspects of the Base Ecclesial Communities in depth of relationship and scope of mission.

Robert Warren, the Archbishop of Canterbury's Adviser on Evangelism in the Decade of Evangelism, refers to the changes that are also taking place in society. He says, 'Society is on a movement from community that didn't work or has broken down. Much of this community related to family and neighbourhood but due to our mobile society, among other things, this has invariably broken down.' He notes, however, that people still value their freedom in the distinct individualistic culture that is prevalent in much of Western civilisation, but suggests that they are beginning to react against this. People still want community and are now making the effort to achieve greater depth in relationships than before.

Maybe this desire for relationship, the forming of community, is in part evidenced by the huge popularity of the soap operas on television. Many people are literally addicted to one or sometimes several soaps each week.

In addition to revealing details of soap stars' personal lives, the tabloid press now panders to this addiction by reporting events that have happened or are about to take place in soaps. These so-called events are portrayed as real news.

Many people, especially the young and restless, desire 'family'. Mike Love, a pastor in Leeds, Yorkshire, identified this need and how it can be met by the implementation of the cell structure within the local church. The cell group becomes family to those in need. A number of the cell groups in his area contain fairly dysfunctional people or at least those who belong to dysfunctional families. In a number of cases, the cell has become a functional family in that a member would contact another cell member to help meet a practical need they have, or to find comfort for the pain and stress they are going through. Mike tells of a lady who recently announced to her group: 'You're my family.' She knew they were there for her, whatever her need.

Most Church leaders accept that the Church is called to meet people's needs and to provide support and love as the family of God. But the question remains whether that is a true description of how the Church operates at present. We have heard many calls to move 'from maintenance to mission'. But can it?

The criticisms levelled at some of the churches in the United States can also be put at the door of British churches. We too have the 'bottleneck' problem: the fear which causes some people to cling to control, the consumer attitude and the lack of desperation for God to be at work.

In a post-Christian society, the challenge is for the churches to spend less time servicing what is already in existence, whether buildings or membership, and more time seeking the lost and addressing the hurts and needs of society. A cell group, with its dual agenda of loving those within the body and loving those outside, is a firm step in the direction of mission while still more than adequately caring for those who are within the body of Christ.

It is many years since anything approaching the dimensions of revival has taken place in Britain, but many suggest that there are some signs that God is at least seeking to prepare his Church for this. Groups such as 'Prayer for Revival' bring together members of all denominations to pray regularly for revival. Church leaders are coming together in cities and towns across the nation to pray. This is unprecedented in the twentieth century. The denominational boundaries are being broken down, and there is some real reconciliation taking place between leaders, with forgiveness for past hurts.

I believe God may be stirring us up to transform our churches into a structure that can at least begin to cope should revival take place. The emphasis upon every-member ministry and the development of leaders is a practical way in which God is mobilising his Church to be ready for any growth he wishes to bring to us.

What God is doing across the continents of the world has, I believe, started to come to us here in Britain. Our spiritual climate might be very different from that experienced in Singapore, Latin America or Africa, but I do believe God wants us to be ready for the change when it comes. Of course, 'changing structures changes structures' and sometimes does no more. However, if God wants us to change our church structures because new life that is to come from him cannot be contained within the old structures, then change structures we must.

CHAPTER 8

DEALING WITH OLD WINESKINS

If you travel east from Bradford city centre along the Wakefield Road, very soon you will see the Elim Pentecostal Church on your right. Half a mile later, at a roundabout, you will see St John's, Bowling, an Anglican church. Then a mile further up this same Wakefield Road you will come to Holme United Reformed Church. Not only are these churches linked by Wakefield Road, but they are also all cell-group churches. Each church has reached the same goal of being a cell-group church through different routes. St John's and Elim were very much aware of what each were doing in this respect, but it came as a surprise when we heard from the pastor of Holme United Reformed Church that it too had now taken steps to become a cell-group church.

Each church was and is different. Elim Pentecostal is an eclectic church which gathers a congregation from across the whole city of Bradford. Holme Church is situated on the edge of the massive Holmewood council estate and has a powerful ministry to the unemployed, both spiritually and practically. All three churches also have their respective denominational distinctions. This suggests that churches of different denominations can all take steps to become cell-group churches.

I am far from qualified to write in detail about other denominations, but I can look at some issues that are raised by my own denominational structures in the Church of England, and can surmise that many of them also apply to other churches. The questions mainly arise in the areas of ecclesiology (the nature of the Church) and missiology (the outreach of the Church). I believe that cell-church principles can be implemented to deal with the present missiological challenges that all churches now face.

What then are some of the crucial ecclesiological issues? For instance, if the cell-group meeting is more than a house group and is a 'new way of being church' the denominational leaders may well ask exactly what it is that people are being invited to join. People concerned for outreach may ask if traditional denominational and parochial ecclesiology is at odds with the vital need to build missionary congregations. Ewan Souter, in a thesis concerning the cell-church movement and Anglicanism, states: 'It is only when we are continually assessing what we are in the light of what we do and vice versa that we can be sure that we are moving on in our grasp of God's revelation to us and in our undertaking of his will for us.'[16] My view is that it is good for the health of any church for these penetrating questions to be asked. We must not rush headlong into a new movement or strategy without asking some searching questions about whether some traditional structures need changing and, if so, what in fact they are being changed into.

Anglicans especially have an implicit commitment to comprehensiveness, which is shown by the widely differing styles of ministry and worship across the Anglican spectrum. The same is true in some other denominations such as Methodism. Would a commitment to cell-group structures and membership be a challenge to this?

Most of the churches that are interested in turning into cell-group churches currently come from the evangelical charismatic wing. They already have a strong emphasis on some foundational principles of cell-group life. For instance, they emphasise personal conversion, discipleship and training. They stress dependence on the Holy Spirit for personal gifting and life in worship. Consequently, when they consider a move to a cell-group structure, they have fewer issues to contend with. Those churches that do not have a vision for lay involvement in pastoral care and mission will find the challenge of a cell-group structure quite daunting.

However, some Anglo-Catholic Anglican churches are exploring cell-group church principles. Many of them are open to charismatic renewal and in their theology share many beliefs with evangelicals. I have already mentioned Base Ecclesial Communities in the context of the church in South America. This movement has grown mainly within the Catholic churches yet the similarities between them and the cell-group churches are clear. This together-ness has meant that representatives both of cell-group churches and Base Ecclesial Communities have joined to lead conferences across Britain, speaking of the benefits to be found in both movements.

Is a cell group a church or (the) church?

Christians who see the cell-group church movement as a threat to a denomination focus on what it means to be 'a church' rather than what it means to be 'church'. This is because for some in the cell-group movement the cell group is regarded as much an expression of the local church as the (Sunday) congregation. It does not matter where the group meets or the size of the meeting. Church is seen to be wherever a group of Christians come together to worship God. The term 'cell-group church' indicates not only a church of cell groups but also that each cell is a church.

Article 19 of the 39 Articles of Faith of the Anglican Church says, 'The visible Church of Christ is a congregation of faithful men in which the pure word of God is preached and the sacraments be duly ministered according to Christ's ordinance in all those things that of necessity are requisite to the same.' Article 25 goes on to say that the sacraments of baptism and Holy Communion are to be celebrated within a church setting, to which I shall return in a moment.

Some in the cell-group church movement argue that the cell group is 'a church' in the way that we have previously accepted the congregational church to be, but they are by no means in the majority. Most would argue that the fundamental aspects of church (such as commitment to Christ, to service, to love, to mission and to worship) are being lived out within the cell group, but the cell groups are also part of a church as well as being church. These are detailed in the service of institution and induction of a vicar. In that service the bishop addresses the members of the congregation, asking them to assent to this commissioning. Members of a cell-group church then live out that commission in the life of their cell group.

Rather than challenging the accepted definition of church, the cell groups are an effective way of mobilising the local church to fulfil its calling and commission. They help to create a community where people also worship and apply the preached word. The cell groups are also natural centres for the prayer life of the local church.

I believe it is also helpful to compare the relationship of the cell group and the local congregation to the relationship of the local congregation and the worldwide Church.

No local church would say it is *the* Church, but is part of the worldwide Church. Most of us acknowledge that this goes way beyond any denominational boundaries. Likewise, the cell group does not see itself as 'the Church' but rather as a part of the local expression of the Church, namely the congregation.

Do cell groups make congregational meetings redundant?

The cell-group church movement emphasises the importance of Christians taking part in the congregational celebratory services. It is there that the vision of the local church is expressed and the biblical teaching is given, both of which are taken back into the cell groups for implementation and application. Therefore the smaller cell group relates to the larger congregation and the Church beyond. I believe this clarifies the relationship between the cell group and the Sunday congregation in ecclesiological terms.

I believe the Church is being called to widen its field of vision while also working out how to be church at the very local level. Sometimes our congregational groupings have missed out on both these aspects by neither being truly community nor having a wider vision beyond the local congregation. Now, by emphasising the cell group as the primary means by which Christians live out their faith in community, and consistently reminding people of our missionary calling, members will want more and more to meet together with people from other cell groups who are also involved in the same mission field covered by the local congregation. In the congregational meeting, the overall vision of the church is given. Also, the Bible is preached to enable the individual Christians within the cells to better live out their faith in their community.

In no way is the cell group making the local congregation meeting redundant. Perhaps in these early years of the cell-group church movement there has been such an emphasis on the importance of attending the cell group that it has appeared that participation in the congregational meeting or celebration is an optional extra. This is in marked contrast to the traditional view that the mid-week house group is an optional extra. Some clergy have suddenly had visions (or nightmares!) of their members joining cell groups which would invariably become separate house churches in a matter of time. The evidence from churches that have developed the cell-group structure shows that this is far from the truth.

The celebration of the sacraments

Articles 19 and 25 of the Church of England indicate that the celebration of the sacraments must be in a congregational setting. Most traditional denominations would agree. It is further prescribed that an ordained priest be present to celebrate Holy Communion or to baptise. Again, many churches have similar provisions, although lay celebration of Holy Communion and baptism is becoming a common practice in some denominations.

As the cell-group members deepen their relationship with one another, it is likely that they will want to celebrate communion within the cell group meeting. Is this a complete impasse, or are there solutions? I believe this matter can be addressed in two ways.

First, Anglican cell-group churches can work creatively within the existing system. Holy Communion can continue to be celebrated within the congregational meeting. As I suggested in chapter 1, a visitor to St John's initially may not know that the church has a cell-group structure. Services are similar in content and style to those that took place prior to our transition. However, if the members of a cell group wish to celebrate communion together in their group setting, they could invite one of the ordained clergy to visit periodically. Another possibility is to have an 'agape meal' which involves the sharing of bread and wine, perhaps within the context of a larger meal, with reference to certain scriptures in the Gospels or 1 Corinthians explaining the work of Jesus on the cross.

Then there is a much more radical and perhaps long-term solution, namely to challenge the tradition as to who is able to say the words of consecration at the Holy Communion service. At present many Anglican dioceses operate a system for 'lay eucharistic assistants' who, after the bread and wine have been consecrated, can take them to those who are sick or house-bound for distribution within that setting. Could any biblical objections be raised to extending that practice to recognise delegated leaders of the church, namely the cell-group leaders?

The debate continues with the question of baptism. However, the issue is not so pressing as many cell-group churches already have the practice of a baptism being undertaken by the clergy and assisted by the cell-group leader. I believe this is a powerful demonstration of the new Christian being baptised into the church within the context of the community of the cell group, but also as part of the wider congregation and the worldwide Church. At St John's I would call on the member's cell-group leader to assist me in the baptism. They also become an additional sponsor to the person baptised. On the occasions in the summer when we have baptised in the local river, it is very helpful to have an extra person with me to help when the river is fast flowing!

The parish system

In the second broad area of missiology the first questions concern the Anglican parish system. In England and

Wales the parish system was established in the time of feudalism. Then the parish priest was an important figure in the local community with a defined responsibility for the pastoral care of that locality. The time has gone when people related primarily to one small geographical area. Today people relate through networks based on how and where they spend their time. What needs to be addressed is the relationship between the cell-group church model for mission that extends beyond a geographical locality, and the local parish church which has pastoral oversight for that area. Robert Warren, writing in *Being Human, Being Church* on the need for the Anglican Church to move from a mode of maintenance to mission, has focused on the urgent need for the Church of England to develop a new missionary focus. He concludes that, in thinking about what it means to be 'a missionary church for the next millennium',[17] the parish system is often an outmoded model.

Having said this, many Anglican clergy are still protective of their local parish area and find it threatening if there are other Anglican groups meeting within its boundaries. In a cell-group church, most newcomers to the cell groups will be those who have a shared interest, activity or other relational tie with existing group members. They may not live within the parent church's parish, and in any case the membership of any particular Anglican church is likely to include a proportion of people who live outside the parish. As these numbers grow, then the logical development is for the cell-group meetings to take place in the homes of people who live outside the parish. Should permission be requested from the vicar of the locality before any such cell-group meeting takes place there?

Social changes have affected the parish system. In our locality, which is partly an urban priority area of the city, sixty per cent of our members still live within the geographical parish. About eighty per cent live within a two-mile radius of the parish church. Because we are in a city, most of the other members live within that city. But put another way, forty per cent of our congregation live in other parishes. As our cell-group meetings move venue with different group members playing host at different times, some cell group meetings will take place in other parishes. Is this threatening to other clergy? Is this undermining the parish system?

In a mainly urban/town setting where there is more affluence, there may be even more social mobility. Consequently, there is even less likelihood of people's relational ties being within a very local area. The general feature of Western society is that we form friendships largely with people from the same socio-economic background. If that is reflected in a particular area of housing, then it is possible that friendships will develop within the locality. However, the determining factor for relational ties is likely to be where we work, where the school is, where the supermarket and the sports centre are located.

In rural areas it appears that the locality is still an important factor in relationships. However, many village communities are no longer the close communities they used to be. In the North Yorkshire village where my mother lives, the vast majority of those who are of working age now work some distance away. All secondary schooling takes place in the local town. The local village shop/post office is not used for most people's primary shopping needs. Again, there is a mixture of relational ties. Some do develop in the locality by being neighbours and by attending village functions. Other friendships develop through the place of work or children's schooling. In addition, the growth of holiday homes has a detrimental effect on community life in some rural areas. People are seen only at weekends and then mostly in the summer months. No deep relationships can be developed.

The cell-group church strategy can fit neatly into the missiology of the parish church, whether it is of the inner city or the urban/town or the rural area. It is based on the real relationships which already exist. It may also stimulate certain cell groups to take up a responsibility for a particular area. Sometimes this is geographical, and sometimes it is an area of need. For instance, a cell group I know of has become involved in the 'soup run' to the homeless in a city centre.

In reality, most clergy have recognised the shortcomings of the parish system, especially in urban and city areas. Little friction is experienced in Bradford when church members cross parish boundaries weekly to attend at their chosen church. In the development of the cell-group church, the congregational meetings and the celebrations can take place in the parish churches, even though cell groups may meet over a wide area. In St John's, Bowling we have three congregational meetings each Sunday, two for adults and one for youth, but all these take place in the parish church.

Fringe membership

Another issue is the effect the cell-group church strategy has on the 'fringe' membership of the church. What about the mission of the church to this fringe? What happens to those who come for a baptism, wedding or funeral, or who belong to a socially oriented mid-week meeting such as an old people's lunch club or a mums and tots group?

There is no reason at all for any of these to fall outside of the cell-group church vision. In fact, here are people who live within the locality and who are approaching the church for a particular service. In reality it is quite likely that either these people are already known to a member of the church, or they at least live in close proximity to some people who are members. Here is an obvious opportunity for relational ties to begin.

In practice, we have tried to use lay members to prepare fringe people for baptisms and weddings. We have also taken steps to introduce the bereaved to church members. Sensitivity is required as the person approaching the church does not always want to be a member of a close cell-group community at this stage. Some wish to be slightly anonymous in their Sunday worship for a period of time. Others do not wish to take their relationship with God any deeper, but just want a wedding in church or 'to have their baby done'. It is important that we have an inclusive approach showing that all are welcome, even though there will be continual invitations and challenges to us all as Christians to be part of a smaller worshipping community in the cell groups.

Church membership

Membership of the Anglican Church is defined as those on the electoral roll. However, emphasis upon attendance at Sunday worship is fast becoming the determining factor at least as far as the calculation of how much the church is to pay to the diocese. The cell-group church model defines church membership as cell membership. In the ideal cell-group church this should present no problem, as all who attend cell groups come together on a Sunday to worship as a congregation, and all who worship as a congregation should be members of a cell group.

Clearly, that is not always the case. However, in many traditionally structured Anglican churches, people who only come to the mid-week communion or only attend the house groups are strictly speaking not seen as part of the church membership if they are not on the electoral roll. There are also some who are on the electoral roll but who never attend. In any event, membership implies more than mere attendance or having a name on a roll. A member also has to accept responsibility within the organisation and to agree to being accountable. Maybe God would have us now move further by seeing as members those who are regularly involved in the vital cell-group meetings.

The authority of leaders

Questions about leadership authority arise over the status of the cell-group leaders. The cell-group leader will be seen to have much more authority than leaders of house groups had in the past. In the cell-group church leaders will be appointed by the senior pastor and the cell-group co-ordinators. In chapter 4 we saw how trainee leaders would also be selected by the cell-group leader and the cell-group co-ordinator. Nevertheless, there is a great awareness within the cell-church movement of the dangers of giving the wrong sort of authority to group leaders.

In certain churches this authority has gone too far and become 'heavy shepherding'. Here group members look to the leader to make decisions for them. These could even include decisions about their job, where they live, or even who they are friends with. These churches are not cell-group churches. The cell-group movement has been anxious to develop a servant leadership rather than any hierarchical model.

R. Greenwood, in *Transforming Priesthood*, argues for the ultimate foundation for authority in Church leadership to be based on the nature of relationships within the Godhead. He writes of how within the triune God, none of the persons is ever in a permanently dominating role. It is easy for us to slip into the world's way of thinking about management structures rather than the biblical concept of equality within the one Church. Greenwood goes on to point out that the 'persons of the Trinity are unique and distinct yet at the same time they are interdependent in a process of mutual love'.[18]

Within the cell-group church movement it is important to stress the equality of all and the servant nature of leadership, especially as some of the diagrammatic representations of the leadership model appear pyramidal and lead to hierarchical thinking.

Certainly the role of the clergy must change if a church is to form cell groups. I covered this in chapter 4. However, there is perhaps a calling to a more apostolic nature of leadership that has been neglected by many clergy. If a cell-group church is to have vision and for that to be regularly put before the leadership (the VHS/VAT meetings) then the clergy must accept and embrace that change and be willing to move from their traditional pastoral role. Ewan Souter in his thesis states that:

> Attitudes to the parish priest are altering in our current climate. Younger people—broadly speaking, those under the age of thirty-five—view their Anglican vicar differently from the older people. More senior members of an Anglican church see the vicar as a 'parson' who has clearly defined pastoral responsibilities, including parish visiting. The younger generations, however, tend to see their minister as a leader and facilitator.

I believe God is calling the leaders of the Church to take the initiative in leading. If the Church is to move from a maintenance mode to one of mission, then the leaders of the Church have to receive a vision from God and seek ways of implementing that vision through his body, the Church. I detect a willingness among many Church members at this time to be led. Of course, there is the risk that positions of leadership will be abused, but that has always been the case. Jesus singled out Peter to lead his Church and we can see that at times Peter deserted his leadership and abused his position (Galatians 2:11–21). Yet Jesus' selection and commissioning of Peter stood.

In this chapter I have examined any areas of potential incompatibility between the cell-group church movement and a traditional denominational church model. I do not think there are any areas of major contention. The reason for this, I believe, is because cell-group church strategy is based upon biblical premises. If there are areas of discrepancy, then I believe the cell-group church movement is a challenge to denominationalism to revert back to its biblical foundations and to live them out in this present age.

CHAPTER 9

THINK BIG,
SO THINK SMALL

On the last day of August 1997, Diana, Princess of Wales, was killed in a car crash in central Paris. There followed unprecedented scenes of mourning across Britain and other parts of the world. The scale of public mourning in Britain took many by surprise. During the week following the death, floral tributes were left at strategic sites across the country. Many thousands of people queued for hours to sign books of condolence. People turned out in their thousands to line the route the cortege would take on the day of the funeral.

During that week, many attended church who had not set foot inside one for years. Some went to special services and some just visited local churches in order to spend some time in quiet to reflect and pray. Many who mouthed the words of the Lord's Prayer in the funeral service had not prayed publicly since childhood.

The spiritual response also took many church leaders by surprise. It appeared that people were not just wanting to express thanks for Diana's life, they also felt a genuine desire to seek God in their grief.

What does this say about people's openness to God at this time? For many years we have accepted that we live in a post-Christian culture where the Church is mainly seen as irrelevant and out of touch. John Stott once famously told of a slogan he had seen written on a wall: 'Jesus yes! Church no!' Maybe today it would read: 'Spirituality yes! Church no!' Even though many people attended church during that week of mourning, attendance figures do not seem to have increased in the months following. Even during the week of mourning, the vast majority of those who publicly demonstrated their grief did not do so in a church. Many said that the most meaningful part of the funeral service was Elton John singing 'Candle in the Wind'. Some have testified to that being a profoundly 'spiritual' experience for them.

Yet Christians know that spiritual reality is to be found in Jesus and *should* be found in his Church. In the West, more and more people are contentedly ignorant of the Christian faith and the content of the Bible. They just do not see the Church as having much to say to them in their everyday lives. It seems culturally remote, and as a result the gospel is consigned to the realms of implausibility and irrelevance. What can be done to stem this decline in influence and open ways for the gospel to be preached and lived out in the reality of everyday life?

If we have been in the Church long enough, we are well aware of people's objections to the Church. For instance, churches are cold, uncomfortable and largely empty. Probably all of us have attended churches like this. It is certainly not just an Anglican problem, as many churches and chapels that were constructed in the last part of the nineteenth century and the early part of the twentieth century to house large congregations are now nearly empty. It is true that pews are not the most comfortable of seats. Many heating systems need turning on at four o'clock on Sunday morning and still make little difference by eleven o'clock. Yet it has to be said that many churches across the land are not like this now. Our church at St

John's, Bowling looks like a traditional Anglican church from the outside, but has been transformed into warm, comfortable meeting areas inside, which are often full. Many congregations now meet in modern school buildings, community halls or even purpose-built, state of the art churches.

Others will say that the Church is only for the middle class. Again, it must be acknowledged that there is some truth in this statement. Robin Gamble, in his book *The Irrelevant Church*, details the failure of the Church to reach the working classes and the normal transforming of working-class people to middle class when they are converted.[19] Yet it is not the whole truth, as there are some churches that are reaching all sections of society. Only recently I visited a church in the centre of Liverpool that had a complete class mix. Our own church is the same—although we don't have any millionaires or brain surgeons yet!

Other objections are that the Church is only for elderly women, the Church is only after your money, churchgoers are hypocrites, church services are boring and use too many books written in archaic language. You may think that those descriptions do not in any way reflect your congregation. However, they are common perceptions from those outside the Church. Rob Warner, in his book *Twenty-first Century Church—Why Radical Change Cannot Wait*, addresses this and says, 'You don't have to go far to hear someone say, "Church? What would I want to go there for?", or even "I wouldn't be seen dead there!"' (although they may well be in time!).[20]

What a contrast this is with the early Church that was perceived by outsiders as dynamic and, it has to be said, threatening. Luke portrays it as a church on the move following the commandment of Jesus, 'You will receive power when the Holy Spirit comes on you; and you will be my witnesses in Jerusalem, and in all Judea and Samaria, and to the ends of the earth' (Acts 1:8). All through the book of Acts there is the balance between the local outworking of church, whether that is in Jerusalem, Antioch, Philippi or Thessalonica, and the mission to the world. Peter leads the local church in Jerusalem in the beginning, but we also see him and Philip, Barnabas and Paul seeking to spread the gospel further afield.

I believe the time has come for the Church in Britain, and in other parts of the Western world, to be willing to take seriously the objections that have been made to the Church as an institution. We must be willing to change that part of the Church over which we have any influence. We must seek to ensure it has a voice into our cultural situation. Primarily this will be done by following the example of the early Church. It will be by proclaiming and living out the gospel in the locality and with an awareness of what the Holy Spirit is doing across the world. We cannot be complacent as obviously the Church is not doing this effectively at this time. We need to listen carefully to what God is saying and wanting us to do in his Church.

God, I believe, is calling us to do this by relationship, by living in Christian community that contrasts with the shallowness of relationships and the lack of community in the world around us. The early Church was not a massive institution that almost had a life of its own. The first Christians made a real priority of Jesus' commandment, 'As I have loved you, so you must love one another' (John 13:34). In the book of Acts, Luke points out three ways in which that commandment was lived out and the fellowship was strengthened: regular contact with each other, the opening of homes to each other, and the sharing of ownership. It was radical and made people sit up and take notice of what the Christians were about.

I honestly believe that it is only through a strategy such as that of cell groups that Christians can live out fully that commandment today. Cell groups are based on relationships, as I have tried to show. They are based on entering into community life. They are about having a vision for mission, seeing neighbours and friends becoming Christians, and then being discipled.

The hand of God?

Bill Beckham, author of *The Second Reformation*,[21] recently shared a helpful illustration of the dynamism and life of the cell group. He used a picture of a hand. The life of the cell group is five-fold, one for each finger.

The thumb is 'Christ in our midst'

This is like the DNA in all our cells. It is Christ who makes the difference, and unless we have encounters with the risen Christ at our cell-group meetings, then we are meeting in vain. Unless Christ is the instigator of the life within the community of the cell group, then we are just another social gathering. I suppose most Christians have gone along to church meetings and nearly forgotten that we are supposed to meet with God there. The old joke which questions whether we would notice if the Holy Spirit had departed from the Church is very apt. Some of us would still be tempted to say, 'It's a bit of a blow, but we'll just have to live with it!'

Instead, we need a dependence upon God that comes before everything else, an acceptance that God really does mean his promise that 'where two or three come together in my name, there am I with them' (Matthew 18:20). One of our youth cell-group leaders was recently telling me how she experienced God making his presence felt in her cell-group meetings. Sometimes the youngsters would come with an attitude of wanting to be entertained but very soon, after a time of prayer, their attitude would change and they would be willing to be used by God for the benefit of others. Sometimes healings took place. Then, perhaps, one would share difficulties they were having in their family and the others would pray for them. They were open to God speaking to them in words and pictures about their everyday situation. They were even willing to experiment with different ways of worshipping God. Christ definitely came among them and made a vast difference.

In one of our adult cell groups recently, a member brought along one of his friends. The friend had been expressing an interest in Christianity and had specifically asked if he could come along to the cell-group meeting. Somewhat reluctantly, the member took him along, a bit afraid that the idea of worshipping and looking at the Bible would put him off. Rather, the reverse happened, as the friend later testified to how amazing it was to have God speaking through others in the group right into his situation. It was not that they actually spoke particular words of advice to him, or even directed what was being said to him, it was just that he knew God was speaking through others into his situation in life at that time.

It is vital for Christians to know that they are meeting with their God. It is also wonderful when those who don't yet believe can visit and 'fall down and worship God, exclaiming, "God is really among you!"' (1 Corinthians 14:25).

The second 'finger' is the cell-group members entering into community and becoming mutually accountable

It is not that we build community, but that we enter into the community that God already has for us. This is an important distinction, as the cell group is not a mutual interest group or a group where members share the same sorts of personalities or do the same sorts of jobs. There is always a temptation to build cell groups where people easily get on with each other (in theory) because they are already friends. Of course, these relationships can and do work sometimes, but there are dangers. One is for the relationship to start to exclude God or, more interestingly, for the element of sacrificial love to be absent. If we already like each other, then we are not as likely to ask God into the relationship to change us or to give us greater understanding of the other person. It is the love that makes a difference. Jesus wants to pour his love into us, not only for each other within the cell group but also for those outside. They will then see the love of Jesus operating among the existing group members to an extent that demonstrates clearly that God is present and active and wants to touch people just like them.

At St John's, we have got nowhere near the level of accountability and sharing as displayed in the early Church. But it is a start to see money changing hands between group members, from those who have to those who are in need. Meals are made for others who are going through times of stress. Visits and phone calls are made because people genuinely want to know how things are with the other group members. This may happen naturally already between friends, but now the cell-group principles promote such attitudes and actions among more people.

Although we are being asked to enter into the community and fellowship that is already established by God for us, there is no doubt we have to work at it. Yet again this is the radical Christianity that speaks into our indifferent world. This is the Church being relevant to people's local needs. A couple of years ago, a woman broke her back falling down the stairs at her home. She was not a member of the church, although her teenage daughter was. Meals were provided for her and her family for months. The result of this was that her perception of 'church' had to change because of her first-hand experience of the body of Christ.

The next 'finger' on the hand is mission

It would make a huge difference to the impact of the Church in Britain if all members of the Church were mobilised in mission. This is possible primarily, I believe, because God's plan is for his Church to be mission-minded. It is difficult to find a theology of Church decline and death. Yet we have ample evidence of a theology of growth and fruit. Jesus may well have assisted the fig tree in its decline and death (Matthew 21), but only because of its lack of growth and fruit. In the cell-group church the paradox of thinking small to grow big is ever before us. We need to look to the formation of small groups within the Church to facilitate the Church in growing to large numbers. As a minister, I do have a desire to see the Church grow, but all the time God is reminding me that the growth depends on strategy for mission held by the cell groups and, behind that, the individual desire a group member will have for seeing those around them come to the Lord. We cannot wave a magic wand and see Church growth. It begins with the individual and the group.

The cell group gives a structure for individuals to reach their full potential in mission. They are then not alone in praying for their relatives, friends, neighbours and workmates. There may well be nine others in the group who are praying regularly for their contacts. Those nine others may also at various times meet with those for whom they are praying. This is joint vision, and an encouragement. The work of outreach is no longer left only to those on the evangelism team or to the minister. It is a shared vision leading to a shared responsibility and a shared privilege.

I have been surprised at who has blossomed in evangelism. A lady who I believed to be slightly on the fringe of the church fellowship soon after joining a cell group surprised the other members and herself by the ease with which she was able to speak with her friends and relatives about what she believed. More than this, she then felt a new confidence to invite other members of her group to meet with them, and to invite them along to events the cell group was organising. It is a bit like the old advert for Heineken lager—she was 'able to reach those that others could not reach'.

As with the other 'fingers', the important factor is reliance and dependence upon God. Jesus himself did only what he [saw] his Father doing' (John 5:19). It is up to God to reveal himself to others, and we must listen to him so that we become aware of just how much he loves them and then get the impetus to continue in prayer for them over the duration. Sometimes this is a very long time. Without God it is impossible to keep going in faithful prayer for them.

The fourth 'finger' is the continuous training and equipping of every member of the Church

This takes place mainly within the cell group itself although there were particular 'encounters' organised centrally during the first year or so. Cell groups are made up of very different people because people are very different! There will be those who have been Christians for some time. They still need to keep on growing as Christians. There will be the new Christians who need some of the basic teaching under their belt in the first year or so. There will be hurting people who need prayer for healing, both so that they can grow in health and so that they can grow in gifting and expertise for the tasks which God wants them to do. There will be dysfunctional members who need particular attention so that God can curb some of their excessive behaviour and place realistic boundaries around their life-style. Then there will be those who need training as apprentice leaders.

I believe that God has a plan to equip and train every Church member, whoever they are. God is always in the business of growing us to be more like him, and giving us the gifts we need so that we will be effective in ministry. He also wants to stretch us beyond what we feel we are humanly capable of. Many gifts are listed in the Bible, such as those in Romans 12, 1 Corinthians 12 or Ephesians 4. Yet in order to use any of these gifts we have to have faith. For example, if God gives us gifts for healing, we still have to take some action, maybe by laying hands on another or by speaking a specific prayer. If we are gifted in administration we have to begin to organise things and sort situations out. We may initially be daunted by the prospect of having to organise an event, but find that once we get into it we have the means to do it effectively.

We miss out on what God has for us because we do not step out in faith. I am probably like most others in desiring to feel in control and comfortable. I am usually in control and comfortable when I have done something before. Therefore to branch out into something new, to venture into the unknown, is unnerving. We are not a cosy social club, but we are here to be equipped and gifted by God into doing his will on earth. The Simon Peter of Luke 5 who said, 'Go away from me, Lord; I am a sinful man!' was transformed into the Simon Peter we see in

Acts 2 and 3, preaching and healing. In between was training and equipping and growing in faith. We too can be transformed.

It is a challenge for the Church today to be about the Father's business, to be able to say, 'We cannot help speaking about what we have seen and heard.' Do we have a testimony that speaks to other people about God? By that I don't mean necessarily our conversion experience, but experience of how we have been taken by God, healed by him, taught by him, trained by him, stretched by him, and become sold out for him.

The fifth 'finger' is of leadership

St John's has many more leaders than I first thought possible. I did not believe in 1993 that by 1997 we would have leaders for our thirty-three cell groups, plus thirty-three apprentice or assistant leaders so that each group could move towards multiplication. Ideally we should also have another sixty-six embryonic trainee leaders waiting in the wings ready for when the groups multiply. We haven't got that far yet, although no doubt God knows who they are. The cell-group church is certainly leader-intensive!

I fully believe it is God's purpose that many within his body, the Church, should become leaders. For too long the Church in Britain has concentrated leadership in the ordained clergy and a few hand-picked lay leaders. Many Church members have become frustrated and disillusioned with the lack of trust placed in them. They have missed out on the opportunity to grow in the Christian life that would have been possible if they had been given some responsibility.

It did not take Jethro long to see that Moses just could not cope with all he was being asked to do as leader of the people of Israel. In Exodus 18:14, we read of his visit to

Moses and, seeing 'all that Moses was doing for the people, he said, "What is this you are doing for the people? Why do you alone sit as judge, while all these people stand round you from morning till evening?"' As part of our leadership training course, we highlight the qualities identified by Jethro for leaders to be appointed. They include teachability, holiness, capability, trustworthiness, honesty and obedience (Exodus 18:21). They were appointed as officials over thousands, hundreds, fifties and tens. That, roughly speaking, is the way of the cell-group church structure. The tens are the cell groups, the fifties are the co-ordinating groups, the hundreds are areas, and in large churches across the world there are leaders over thousands. In this model, the leadership is taken closer to the individual. They are in touch with the situation and needs of the people. They know what is going on in their lives and the pressures they are under.

What a contrast to the way Church leaders are usually portrayed in the media, and especially on television! Vicars are invariably portrayed as weak, ineffective characters who are out of touch with the modern world. If any appear in the newspapers, it is usually due to some peculiar theological views, or because they have sinned sexually. If it grieves me to see the portrayal of Church leaders in this way, how much more it must grieve God to see his Church portrayed in this way, exemplifying its supposed irrelevance to the world. No doubt there is some truth behind the caricatures. There are Church leaders who seem out of touch with life in the 1990s and others who are maybe too in touch with it! Yet this is not how it should be.

I praise God for our leaders in St John's. Many of them would be spurned by the world as leaders. Many of them have fallen foul of the education system. Many have 'exciting histories'. Many had little self-esteem at the point when God chose them. And yet these are the leaders I believe God has chosen to be his Church in the world. They can prove that Jesus is concerned with the needs of the world and is ready to act. Listen to what some of them say:

'God led me to believe that he wanted me to share my experience, strength and hope with others who were suffering . . . I also knew quite early in my Christian life that God, through my evangelism and testimony, would reach people outside the group structure, eg family, friends, workmates.'

'It's not that I am especially talented in any way to be the leader of my small group. I see others more able and confident in worldly terms, even within my group, than myself. It's more that I knew in my heart more or less from the beginning of my Christian walk with God that at some point I would be a leader. God has given me vision for the group, and shows me what he is doing in the group at certain times. He has also given me the heart to pray and intercede for individuals within the group.'

'It became clear to us as a couple that God had called us to leadership. He kind of fast-forwarded us through lots of healing and sorting. We just went for it and gave up everything (including hopes of living abroad!). Three or so years down the road we are both leaders and the Lord has totally blessed us.'

'God gave me what I would call a servant heart. In effect, he said, "Be faithful in the little things." So for many years I did things like washing up, putting chairs out, cleaning the church and even the toilets. But then I found the church leaders were asking me to become a Sunday school teacher, then a youth leader, and latterly a churchwarden, an adult group leader, and a member of the eldership team. All this time God has been doing a lot of inner healing in my life, teaching me a lot about myself and others. For much of this time I was working in industry. This was the best theological college for me.'

'I really needed to believe that leadership was what God wanted me to do . . . it was so different to what I would have expected to be doing. In fact, it was a case of stepping out and doing it, trusting that God would be with me. Several years on, I can say that he definitely has been there, and how essential this knowledge has been.'

Called to a battle

I am under no illusion that radical change for the Church is difficult. We know God spoke to us in 1992/93 about the change that should take place in our structure at St John's, Bowling. We have tried to obey, and along the way we have struggled to become a church that is more aware of the world around and with a message that speaks into people's specific situations. Sometimes our hearing has not been good and we have missed what God was really saying. At other times we have been slow to change, want-ing to hold on to the familiar and the comfortable. At other times we have found ourselves in the thick of spiritual warfare. This must not be underestimated.

Whenever I read Jesus' prayer in John 17, I am struck by the emphasis on protection for his disciples: 'Holy Father, protect them by the power of your name' (11); 'While I was with them, I protected them' (12); 'My prayer is not that you take them out of the world but that you protect them from the evil one' (15). As Jesus interceded for his disciples collectively and for Peter specifically (Luke 22:32), so I believe we need his intercession for us at this time. The spiritual warfare takes many forms.

Over the years we have seen the leadership battered and,

in some cases, taken out. Leaders have been tempted to make wrong choices in their lives. Others have had difficulties in their secular jobs. Battles have been fought against the lies of low self-esteem. Conflicts have arisen over minor issues. Cell-group members have been distracted from God's purpose for them by the temptation to 'serve the Lord elsewhere'. They later came to see they had been wrong in going.

It's not only the leaders that have suffered. I believe another strategy of the evil one has been to bless a cell group with a disproportionate number of dysfunctional people! It has been necessary to make some cell groups aware that the actions of a dysfunctional person in their group are not always to be accepted and put up with. A cell group can so easily be destroyed while such a person makes themselves at home within the group. We have to devise strategies to see healing come to those who are domineering, destructive, demanding, passive or over-religious. The evil one is very good at making Christians feel guilty about their lack of tolerance for unacceptable behaviour!

It is my firm belief that God is renewing his Church across the world. In many ways we in the West are having to catch up with what God is doing elsewhere. Whether this is out of complacency and a false belief that we are a 'Christian country', I am not sure. It is certainly necessary for us to see that the Church in the West needs now to be a missionary Church with a readiness to live out the gospel in an effective, relevant manner.

Yet I do believe that God is at work in Britain at this time. There is an air of change in the spiritual climate; a confident feel rather than a retiring, apologetic atmosphere. God has called large numbers of Christian leaders to intercede for their areas, and to link up with leaders of churches in other denominations and groupings to do this.

There is a belief in the power of God being released through this unity to change things.

There is a recognition that, whereas many people in the world around us have needs, existing societies, institutions and structures are not able to meet those needs fully. As I write, the Government and various agencies are foundering in trying to counter the epidemic of drug-taking among young people. Even if there are effective detoxification and rehabilitation centres, the problems will not be fully solved unless the underlying needs of the youngsters are addressed. Only God can do this, and Christians across the country are rising to the challenge of fighting social needs with God-centred strategies. There is confidence that this can change things.

The Church is being called to rise up and change and be relevant for people in our localities, but also in speaking into the issues affecting all countries. For the Church to take up the cell-group structure is not the whole answer, but I believe it is part of the answer. It transforms the Church on a local level to be a mobilised Church. It is part of the army of God taking ground back from the evil one that has for so long remained undisputedly in possession.

At St John's we are committed to this transition into cell groups. We are certainly not there yet, but we are committed to making whatever changes are necessary in order to be effective in the five 'fingers' as outlined before. I think when we began in 1993 I felt the transition would take two or three years. Four years down the road, I now believe the time scale is much more like seven to ten years. We have seen some cell groups multiply and others having to be reconstituted. We have seen some amazing growth in our youth work, but also some of the growth frustrated because we do not have enough leaders. Sometimes it has felt like we are taking two steps forward, only then to take one large step back. We are nevertheless committed to this change, to this transition into a cell-group church.

I leave you with this question. Has God spoken to you about making this change in the structure of the church of which you are a part? Praise God that it is Jesus who says, 'I will build my Church.' My prayer is that we do not get in his way!

NOTES

1. Cleverley, Charlie, *Church Planting, Our Future Hope* (Scripture Union, 1991).
2. Neighbour Jnr, Ralph, *Where Do We Go from Here?* (Touch Publications, 1990).
3. *Ibid.*
4. Peterson, Jim, *Evangelism as a Lifestyle* (Navpress, 1980).
5. Lee, David, and Schluter Michael, *The R Factor* (Hodder and Stoughton, 1993).
6. Neighbour Jnr, Ralph, *op. cit.*
7. George, Carl, *Prepare Your Church for the Future* (Revell: Grand Rapids, MI, 1995).
8. Croft, Steve, *Growing New Christians* (Marshall Pickering, 1993).
9. Beckham, Bill, article in *Cell Church Magazine* (Touch Publications, 1992).
10. Neighbour Jnr, Ralph, *Cover the Bible* (Touch Publications, 1991).
11. Egli, Jim, and Hoer, Ben, *I Factor* (Touch Publications, 1993).
12. Hybels, Bill, *Too Busy Not To Pray* (IVP, 1988).
13. Yonggi Cho, David (Paul), *Successful Home Cell Groups* (Bridge Publishing, 1981).
14. *Ibid.*

15. Freestone, Ian, *A New Way of Being Church* (Sold Out Publications, 1995).

16. Souter, Ewan, unpublished thesis.

17. Warren, Robert, *Being Human, Being Church* (Marshall Pickering, 1995).

18. Greenwood, R., *Transforming Priesthood* (SPCK: London, 1994).

19. Gamble, Robin, *The Irrelevant Church* (Monarch: Crowborough, 1991).

20. Warner, Rob, *Twenty-first Century Church* (Hodder and Stoughton: London, 1993).

21. Beckham, Bill, *The Second Reformation* (Touch Publications, 1993).